Miscellanea Hasaitica

TO THE MEMORY OF HENRY FIELD

CNI PUBLICATIONS 9

MISCELLANEA HASAITICA

BY D.T. POTTS

THE CARSTEN NIEBUHR INSTITUTE OF ANCIENT NEAR EASTERN STUDIES
UNIVERSITY OF COPENHAGEN · 1989 · MUSEUM TUSCULANUM PRESS

D.T. POTTS, MISCELLANEA HASAITICA
The publication of this book was made possible
by grants from Statens Humanistiske Forskningsråd and
C.L. Davids Fond og Samling.

Cover designed by Thora Fisker.

Set on a Linotronic 300 by Maczine, Copenhagen,
and printed by Special-Trykkeriet Viborg a/s, 1989.

Published and distributed by Museum Tusculanum Press,
University of Copenhagen, Njalsgade 94
DK - 2300 Copenhagen S.

ISBN 87-7289-068-1
ISSN 09202-5499

Contents

Preface and Acknowledgements

In 1977 I paid my first visit to the Eastern Province of the Kingdom of Saudi Arabia. Since that time I have never ceased to be fascinated by the archaeology and history of the region known traditionally as al-Hasa. More than half a dozen archaeologists had, of course, preceded me, including P.B. Cornwall, H. Field, P.V. Glob, T.G. Bibby, A.H. Masry, R.McC. Adams, McG. Gibson, J. Zarins, and C. Piesinger, while the historian R. Stiehl had also made several forays into the area. But the real exploration of al-Hasa was not accomplished by them, still less by me. That was the work of dozens of ARAMCO employees and their families, for the most part resident in Dhahran, who had over the years traversed the entire province in search of antiquities, and thus come to know many sites which had been destroyed by the time teams of archaeologists were eventually sent out by the Saudi Arabian Department of Antiquities. This casual exploration of al-Hasa went on year after year, every Friday of the week, and the yield of important sites and finds was correspondingly great.

I have been fortunate in meeting many of those who were engaged in this exploration. John Seip, who worked in oil-well maintenance from the late 1940's until the early 1970's, drove from well to well on his inspection tours when there were almost no paved roads in the area, and largely avoided them once they had been built. In this way, he covered ground which few archaeologists have ever been over, and discovered sites which have not been revisited since. Grace Burkholder, a former school teacher in Dhahran, discovered the first examples of painted Ubaid pottery while out on her Friday excursions. James P. Mandaville, Jr., a keen student of pre-Islamic inscriptions before his botanical interests got the better of him, photographed many texts at Thaj, Ayn Jawan, and Qatif. The late Thomas Barger, one-time president of ARAMCO, together with his family, made numerous discoveries at Thaj and on the Dhahran Airport site, as well as at more distant al-ʿUla and Madain Salih. Many more names could be cited, but these few examples suffice to illustrate that the finds made over the years were both numerous and important.

One can hardly overestimate the extreme interest which the scholarly community took in the discoveries made by ARAMCO members, the more so as Saudi Arabia had always been difficult of access to scholars. Many individuals, such as Jim Mandaville, Tom Barger, Grace Burkholder, and Marny Golding, carefully documented the findspots of their material and communicated the nature of it to academics in Europe and America. This kind of generous cooperation, before the existence of an active Department of Antiquities in Riyadh, led directly to a number of publications in which objects and inscriptions from the Eastern Province were treated by scholars outside of Saudi Arabia (e.g. Jamme 1966, Bibby 1973, Sordinas 1973 and 1978, Potts 1986a, Edens 1988, Lombard 1988). In addition, several members of the ARAMCO community, self-taught but active and committed, made significant contributions over the years to the literature on the archaeology and early history of al-Hasa (e.g. Mandaville 1963, Barger 1965 and 1969, James 1969, McClure 1971, Burkholder and Golding 1971, Burkholder 1971, 1972, 1974, and 1984, Golding 1974 and 1984), while at least two important doctoral theses used the research of ARAMCO amateurs as a springboard (Masry 1974, Piesinger 1983). But the finds dealt with in these publications represent only the tip of an enormous iceberg, inappropriate as this metaphor may be for describing conditions in the Arabian peninsula. Many more discoveries have never been transmitted for fear that if their existence became known they would have to be surrendered to the Museum of Archaeology and Ethnography in Riyadh, which opened in 1976. On the other hand, just as many important finds had long since left Saudi Arabia by the time the Department of Antiquities began to operate, and these have for the most part been retained by the families which found them, although some objects have been sold and found their way into both public and private collections.

My own interest in this material developed in a roundabout way. While working at Thaj in 1983, I became aware of the existence of several private collections of coins which had been found there. These, it appeared, far outnumbered the very modest number of coins then known from the site. In contacting individuals with coins, I gradually built up a correspondence with many former ARAMCO employees, and learned of numerous non-numismatic finds of importance from various sites of all periods. The steady flowof photographs and the maintenance of this correspondence has been constant over the years, with the result that I have gradually accumulated a sizable store of material. It was once my intention to publish all of the Eastern Province material, both coins and objects, along with historical chapters, in the form of a single monograph. While working on *The Arabian Gulf in Antiquity,* however, I found that much of the historical content of my projected Eastern Province monograph belonged in the larger synthesis of Gulf archaeology and history. Thus, I abandoned the idea of a single Eastern Province study, and decided to compile all of the coins which I had been able to document from the area, along with others from the Oman peninsula, into a monograph on *The Pre-Islamic Coinage of Eastern Arabia.* As I was assembling the photographic illustrations for *The Arabian Gulf in Antiquity,* I realized that my stock of miscellaneous finds from the Eastern Province was sufficiently large to warrant a separate, if less ambitious publication than the original monograph which I had once planned to devote to the area. *Miscellanea Hasaitica* is the result.

This miscellany is nothing more than an essay on finds from al-Hasa which their owners have been kind enough to draw to my attention over the past five years. The quality of the photographs is highly variable. In most cases I have neither exact measurements nor precise descriptions, although the findspots of the majority of the pieces illustrated are known. Yet the relative dearth of material from al-Hasa, coupled with the extreme interest of some of these pieces, makes their publication now, if only in a summary fashion, desirable. Scholars active in Near Eastern archaeology, particularly in the Arabian Gulf region, will, I feel sure, require no lengthy commentary on the objects illustrated to convince them of the inherent interest of such a large number of objects from what is still essentially *terra incognita*. This is meant neither as an excuse for sloppy scholarship on my part, nor for lack of sufficient interest to document the finds further. But the delays which the amplification of the documentation would entail, not to mention the costs involved if I were to try to see and re-photograph each and every one of these finds, argues against adopting such an approach. Rather, I feel certain that my colleagues will be grateful to see this material at the earliest possible date.

My thanks are indeed great to all who have helped me over the years. Some wish to remain anonymous, and to them I express my sincerest appreciation. This publication, however modest, should be taken by them as a token of my esteem. The late Marny Golding and the late Tom Barger deserve a special word of thanks. Bert Golding, Teresa Barger, Jim Mandaville, Paul and Elizabeth Arnot, John Seip, Bob Morris, Bob Maby, and Hal McClure have all helped in numerous ways. Both Beatrice de Cardi and Jean-François Salles were kind enough to read an earlier draft of this work, and I am particularly grateful to the latter for his many comments and suggestions. Finally, it is a great pleasure to acknowledge with thanks the generous subventions towards the cost of publishing this monograph which were granted by the Danish Research Council for the Humanities, and the C.L. David Foundation and Collection.

Most of the material illustrated here was collected before there was a Department of Antiquities in Riyadh.. Had it not been picked up at the time, there is little doubt that it would have disappeared, for urban development in the Eastern Province during the past two decades has been so great that vast stretches of the natural and archaeological landscape have been obliterated in the course of constructing highways, housing, and all manner of commercial and industrial establishments. We must be grateful to the ARAMCO community, to those named above and those who wish to remain anonymous, for saving this material for scholarship.

The text of this monograph was written during November and December, 1988, and was revised slightly just before submission to the printer in September, 1989.

Copenhagen D.T. POTTS

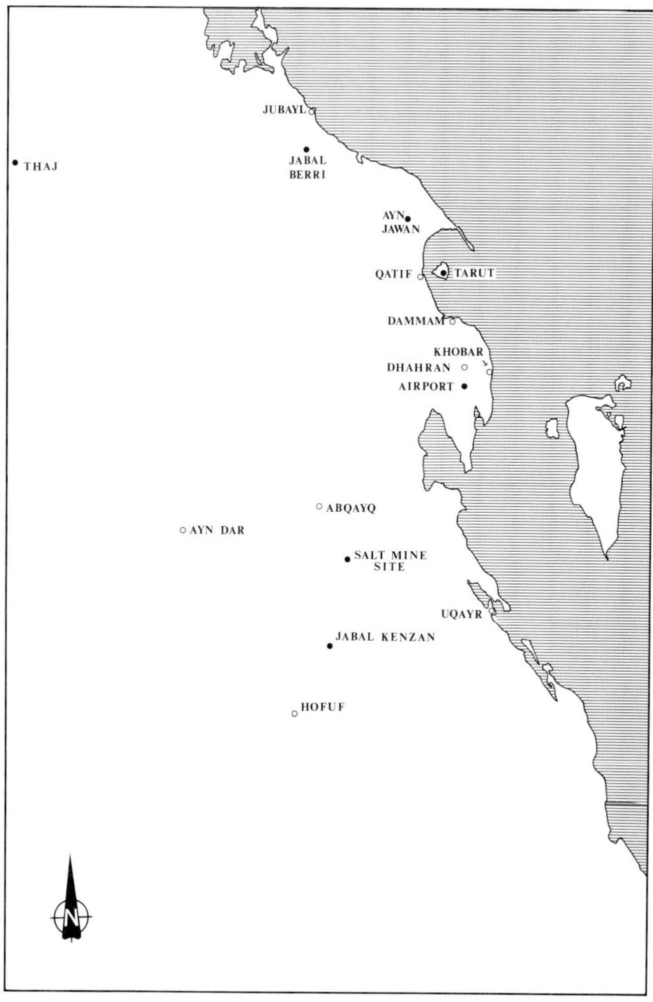

Fig. 1. Map of the area discussed in the text.

Organization of the Present Work

To the Western observer, northeastern Arabia is a desert zone comprised of two main oases - al-Hasa and Qatif - and a number of inhabited off-shore islands. In the eyes of its native inhabitants, however, it has always possessed a far more varied topography. This is perhaps best reflected by the fact that no fewer than twenty-two indigenous names were used at the beginning of this century to denominate separate tracts of land in al-Hasa (Lorimer 1908:659).

The material presented in this volume comes from sites which are spread over five of the traditional sub-divisions of the area, as well as from one of its major islands. Moving from north to south, we have finds from Thaj in the Wadi al-Miyah; from the area of Jabal Berri in region known as Biyadh; from Tarut island; from Dammam in the Qatif Oasis area; from Dhahran and al-Khobar in the Barr-adh-Dhahran zone; and from Jabal Kenzan and the so-called Salt Mine Site, in the al-Hasa, i.e. Hofuf/Mubarraz oasis, area. The presentation of the finds here will not, however, follow a geographical arrangement. Rather, it seems more convenient for the reader if they are presented chronologically. We shall begin with the earliest finds, of third millennium date, and work our way up to the Sasanian period.

Fig. 2. Buffware jar with shoulder lugs found between Dammam and al-Khobar.
Fig. 3. Buffware jar with straight spout from the Dhahran Airport site.

The Third Millennium

CHAPTER I

The development of al-Hasa during the early third millennium was more advanced than has generally been acknowledged. At a time when Bahrain seems to have had little significant occupation, settlements flourished on Tarut, around Abqayq, outside of Hofuf, and as far south as Yabrin. That these communities were in touch with the wider world is amply demonstrated by the imported material which has been found in the region.

Elsewhere I have published a drooping buffware spout from the Dhahran area (Potts 1986a:Pl. 1b) which resembles Mesopotamian pottery of the Late Uruk period. The earliest foreign pieces illustrated here are a pair of vessels from the Dammam-Dhahran-al-Khobar triangle. Both point clearly to the existence of contact with southern Mesopotamia.

One of these pieces (Fig. 2), a buffware jar with a high, carinated shoulder, no neck, and two nose-lugs still visible, was found between Khobar and Dammam. It is 9 cm. tall, and has a base diameter of 5.7 cm. It resembles a type attested in Mesopotamia during the Jamdat Nasr period (e.g. Delougaz 1952:Pl. 22e = Protoliterate c-d type B.455.253; Pongratz-Leisten 1988:262, no. 314; Woolley 1955:Pl. 60, type JN. 101, cf. Vértesalji and Kolbus 1985:108).

The other jar (Fig. 3) is a badly worn buffware vessel with rounded rim, short neck, and straight spout. The body is ovoid; the base slightly rounded. The vessel stands 21.8 cm. high; has a rim diameter of 7.1 cm.; and a base diameter of 7.7 cm. It was found on the large site south of the Dhahran Airport (cf. Potts et al. 1978:15-18). Although badly preserved, this vessel would seem to resemble most closely a well-known type of Mesopotamian spouted jar common in the ED I period (cf. Delougaz 1952:Pl. 38a-b, types C.556.242 and C.545.242; Nissen 1970:Taf. 64:13/13, Taf. 69:18/36, Woolley 1955:Pl. 64, JN. 166).

The bulk of the third millennium finds presented here come, however, from the island of Tarut. Situated c. 3.2 km. east-north-east of Qatif, the island has traditionally been accessible from the mainland via a ford which is passable at low-tide (a modern causeway now connects the island to the mainland). In northeastern Arabia, population centers have only grown up, and intensive date cultivation has only been possible, where hand-dug wells or natural springs have brought water from the region's rich aquifers to the surface (cf. Potts 1984:89-94). In this regard, Tarut has been favored by the presence of two natural springs located near the center of the island, 'Ain al-Hammam and 'Ain Umm al-Fursan, the water of which has always been considered excellent

(Lorimer 1908/II:1872). Date cultivation and pearl-diving were the traditional occupations of the island's population which, at the beginning of this century, was a mixture of local Bani Khalid, Sadah, and Junaidat *bedu* (*Sunni*); Baharinahs, originally hailing from Bahrain (*Shi'ah*); and Bani Yas of the Al Bu Falasah section (*Sunni*), from Abu Dhabi.

Early in 1966 a large quantity of objects, dating principally to the third millennium and the Seleucid-Parthian period, emerged from a mound near al-Rufayah, a village c. 1.5 km. southeast of Tarut town. T.G. Bibby has described this event briefly, noting that "a number of objects of an intriguing nature had been turning up in the course of breaking in new ground for gardens" (Bibby 1973:29), although elsewhere he suggested that the finds were made "in the course, it is said, of road-building" (Bibby 1973:31). P.V. Glob and Bibby had visited the site in 1964, describing it as "an area of low sandy mounds...where considerable quarrying of sand was in process" (Bibby 1966:150). The need for sand in this particular case was prompted by the construction of the causeway which now connects Tarut to Qatif (Zarins 1978:65; cf. Rashid 1972:160 who notes only that earth and stone was removed "um das Niveau zu ebnen").

Spurred by the Tarut discoveries, photographs of which had been sent by T. Barger to Bibby early in 1966, the Danish expedition carried out three brief soundings at the site two years later, although the material recovered was in no way comparable in quality or quantity to that which had been found previously at the site. In view of the extreme importance of these finds, it is fortunate that we now possess an "eye-witness account" by P. Arnot, a former Vice-President of ARAMCO, who was resident in Dhahran at the time, visited the site on several occasions, and was himself present when photographs of the most important objects were taken. I would like to express my sincere thanks to the Barger family, particularly Teresa Barger, for giving me a set of the Tarut photographs for study. As much of what P. Arnot has described pertains to the later, Seleucid-Parthian graves on the site, this will be omitted here but can be found in Chapter IV. I have inserted my own clarifications in brackets <> when appropriate.

Arnot writes (1986a):

> "I was present when the pictures of the Tarut Island objects were photographed in a local official's office on the Island....I am reasonably sure that most of the objects photographed were recovered from a burial mound located near the coast a few miles <c. 1.5 km.> east of the old fort area <Tarut town>. The mound when I first saw it was about four to six feet <1-2 m.> in thickness resting on top of a calcareous shelly-sandy rock. The top material of the mound was essentially coarse sand and small shells which the locals (unfortunately) were mining and hauling away by donkey carts - later mechanical equipment was used. The mound area was roughly about

Fig. 4. Basket-shaped soft-stone bowls from Tarut.
Fig. 5. Biconical jar with everted rim from Tarut.

seventy by three hundred feet <c. 20 x 100 m.> in area and stood out from the surrounding terrain....The surface of the already mined area of the mound contained small pieces of alabaster, steatite, plain pottery and glazed pottery shards, all representative of the photographed vessels. The presence of these shards supports my contention that the photographed vessels and some of the headstones <cf. Chapter IV> most likely were recovered from this burial mound".

The earliest finds which can, with certainty, be attributed to this precise area date to the Early Dynastic period. Several objects, although previously published elsewhere, are illustrated again here so as to give the reader a better impression of the totality (however fragmentary) of finds which were collected in 1966. To begin with, we find a large group of undecorated, basket-

Fig. 6. Nude male statue from Tarut.

shaped steatite bowls (Fig. 4). T.F. Potts (n.d.) has called these "bag-shaped goblets" (Fig. 4, left and center) and "square-based cylindrical goblets" (Fig. 4, right). Based on the recently revised chronology of the Jamdat Nasr cemetery at Ur (Vértesalji and Kolbus 1985), these can be assigned to the Early Dynastic II period (cf. Potts 1986a:149, with refs. to relevant pieces catalogued in Zarins 1978). A biconical jar (Fig. 5) with rounded body and everted rim (cf. Potts 1986a:Pl. 2a, Fig. 7:1) resembles Mesopotamian pottery dating to late ED I and II-III (Vértesalji and Kolbus 1985:108, for Ur Jamdat Nasr cemetery type 56; Delougaz 1952:Pl. 74m, type B.545.540; cf. Pongratz-Leisten 1988:216, nr. 103). Another find which has been dated to the Fara period or ED II is the by now well-known statue (Fig. 6) of a standing nude male with hands clasped in a traditional Sumerian devotional posture (cf. Rashid 1972, Potts 1986a:146 and Pl. 3, with earlier literature). As this piece has recently been treated again in greater detail elsewhere (Potts, in press a), we will pass over it quickly, but it should be noted that three incised lines on the belly of the figure recall the triple girdle worn, for example, by a nude male figure on a cast copper

Fig. 7. Plain soft-stone bowl from Tarut.
Fig. 8. Cylindrical soft-stone goblet with concave profile from Tarut.
Fig. 9. Base of a cylindrical soft-stone goblet from Tarut.

offering stand of ED II date from temple oval I at Khafajah (Frankfort 1939:41, No. 181), or on an alabaster statue of a nude, bearded male standing in much the same attitude as that of the Tarut statue, from Umma (Spycket 1981:56-57, Fig. 20). Attention is also drawn to the incised V on the chest and the barely visible incised strokes beneath it. This appears to represent a ribbon or piece of cloth worn around the neck, although there is no indication on the back of the figure's neck that the decoration was continuous. The photograph of the statue, taken from the right side, is published here for the first time, but according to P. Arnot, the statue did not originate with the rest of the Tarut material which appeared in 1966 (Arnot 1986a).

Several more pieces are published here which can be assigned an Early Dynastic II or II-III date. These include a plain steatite bowl with five drill holes made when it was repaired in antiquity (Fig. 7, previously illustrated in Zarins 1978:Pls. 64:86 and 75:86). T.F. Potts (n.d., n. 66) classifies this as a "sub-conical, slightly concave profile bowl", and points to a close parallel with type 28 in the Jamdat Nasr cemetery at Ur (Woolley 1955:Pl. 65), dating to late ED I and II (Vértesalji and Kolbus 1985:107, cf. Potts, n.d., n. 68).

In the category of what T.F. Potts has called "concave profile, cylindrical goblets" we can place a complete steatite vessel which, although rather short for the designation "goblet", conforms to the type as presently defined. The example shown here (Fig. 8) has a base diameter of 8.6 cm.; a rim diameter of 9.5 cm.; and is 4.5 cm. tall. Many parallels exist for this type of vessel. A nearly identical example is known from Shahdad, where the taller variety is also found (Hakemi 1972:Pl. IXA and XB). Similar pieces have also been found, for example, in Tomb A at Hili North (Vogt 1985:Pl. 27:11); in the great tomb at Hili (Frifelt 1971:Fig. 3B); in Cairn I on Umm an-Nar island (Thorvildsen 1963:Fig. 21); at Tepe Yahya (Lamberg-Karlovsky 1970:Pl. 26A); and in the Jamdat Nasr cemetery at Ur (Woolley 1955:Pl. 34, U.19213a). These finds all converge to suggest a late third millennium date, perhaps c. 2300-2100 B.C.

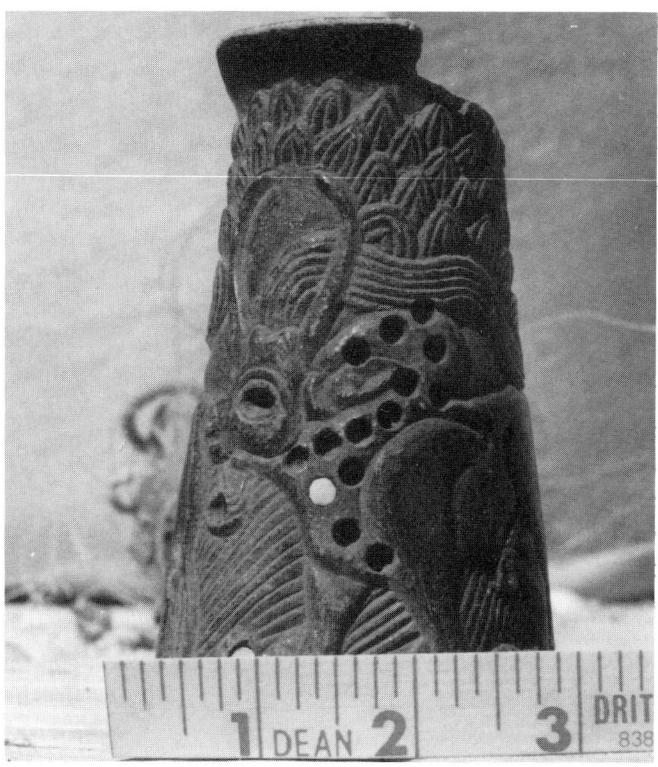

The base of a second example of the same type from Tarut is also published here (Fig. 9).

Hundreds of carved soft-stone vessels with figurative or patterned designs, belonging to the *série ancienne*, have also been recovered from Tarut. Many of these have been published over the years (e.g. Burkholder 1971 and 1984; Kohl 1974), and a full catalogue of the Museum of Archaeology and Ethnography's holdings in Riyadh has been available for some time (Zarins 1978). One of the most elaborate pieces (Fig. 10) from the area is an 11.4 cm. tall beaker with a pair of horned, humped bulls shown striding beneath stylized vegetation. Circular mother-of-pearl inlays, several of which are still in situ, adorned the hump, eyes, and dewlap of the bull. The piece, now in a private collection, has recently been on loan to the Metropolitan Museum of Art in New York, and is included in a work by H. Pittman on Bronze Age art from Iran, Central Asia and the Indus Valley. There it is described as being "reportedly from the region of the Gulf" (Pittman 1984:22). The provenance of the piece is, however, without any doubt, Tarut, and this has long been established (cf. Kohl 1974:168 and Pl. XLVa, Burkholder 1984:Pl. 10-11, for earlier treatments of the vase).

Fig. 10 (left). ***Série ancienne*** **soft-stone beaker from Tarut.**

Fig. 11 (right, upper). ***Série ancienne*** **soft-stone jar from Tarut.**

Fig. 12 (right, lower). Base of a ***série ancienne*** **soft-stone canister from Tarut.**

Two further pieces published here belong to the *série ancienne*. The first (Fig. 11) is 7.1 cm. tall; has a base diameter of 7.5 cm.; and a rim diameter of just slightly less. The rim flares slightly and is offset from the vessel's flat shoulder. The surface of the shoulder is decorated with a pattern of symmetrically opposed, hatched triangles (cf. Kohl 1974:187 for the use of this decorative convention). The body, on the other hand, is decorated with eleven concentric rows of slanting, slightly raised rectangles, each row slanting in the opposite direction of the one above it to create a herringbone pattern. A vessel which resembles this in general shape, although it was more squat and had a damaged rim, was found at Tepe Yahya in 1969 (Lamberg-Karlovsky 1970:Pl. 26C; 1988:Fig. 3A). The decoration on the shoulder of the Yahya exemplar consists of a band of cross-hatching, while the body of the vessel shows an overall pattern of small, pendant, incised triangles, arranged in concentric rows. The vessel was originally assigned to Period IVB, although Kohl later attributed it to Period IVA (Kohl 1974:81 and Pl. XIXa). Unfortunately, the context from which the Yahya piece derives (BW TT5 5), while rich in *série ancienne* steatite and painted pottery, was poor in architecture and could never be properly correlated with the rest of the statigraphy on the site (Potts 1980:252). Nevertheless, judging by the associated ceramics, the piece should be dated to the late third millennium, and a similar date can therefore be suggested for the Tarut vessel.

The final piece of *série ancienne* steatite presented here (cf. Anonymous 1975:148 center) is the base of a canister or shallow, straight-sided bowl (Fig. 12). It is decorated with what Kohl has called the "bevelled square" (Kohl 1974:196), a design which resembles brickwork. An incised line can be seen running along the base of the vessel. Above this is a register of seven rows of bevelled squares. Another raised line most probably divided the decorative pattern of the vessel here, and accounts for the even break in the vessel wall at this point. These traits allow us to identify this as the base of a type well-known at Susa (Miroschedji 1973:Pl. IIk), Nippur (Kohl 1974:Pl. LVIIa), and Tepe Yahya (Kohl 1974:Pl. LVIIb; Lamberg-Karlovsky 1988:Fig. 3K).

A number of interesting calcite or alabaster vessels were also recovered from the mound at al-Rufayah. Although very simple in shape, two of the small, open bowls illustrated here can be compared with finds from Mesopotamia. The shallow bowl with curving sides in Fig. 13 recalls Jamdat Nasr cemetery shapes JN 13 and 14. These occur in Jamdat Nasr/ED I, and Jamdat Nasr through ED II period graves at Ur, respectively (Vértesalji and Kolbus 1985:107). A slightly deeper bowl with straighter sides of banded calcite or alabaster (Fig. 15) might be compared to Jamdat Nasr cemetery shapes JN 19 or 20, both of which are attested from the Jamdat Nasr through the ED II period (Vértesalji and Kolbus 1985:107). Two more plain, shallow bowls (Figs. 14 and 16) are illustrated here, but it is not certain from the photographs whether these are made of calcite or steatite. The fact that they are opaque would suggest that the material is in any case different from that which we see in Figs. 13 and 15. The shape of these vessels is so simple that it would be hazardous to press a particular date. They could be as early as the other two, but in describing several much later cist graves (cf. Chapter IV) in the same mound, P. Arnot noted that alabaster vessels were found there as well. Thus, it is equally possible that these vessels date to a much later period. In this connection it would be well to recall that the Iron Age graves at al-Qusais, in Dubai, and al-Hajjar, on Bahrain, yielded a number of calcite or alabaster jars, cups and bowls (Lombard 1979:100 and Pls. LXXVI-LXXVII; 1985:104 and Fig. 41:116-117).

Another calcite or alabaster vessel form of undoubted late third millennium date is, however, attested in the Tarut collection. G. Burkholder has published a tall, conical vessel from Tarut, made of what she termed "travertine marble" (Burkholder 1984:Pl. 29a). Elsewhere, I have noted that two vessels of this type were found on Tarut, and that further examples were known from Ur, Tello, and the Barbar temple on Bahrain (Potts 1986b:283-284). T.F. Potts, who classifies this type as "tall cylindrical vases with straight or slightly convex profile and everted rim", has now collected no fewer than ten examples inscribed

Fig. 13. Calcite or alabaster dish from Tarut. Fig. 14. Stone bowl from Tarut.

Fig. 15. Stone bowl from Tarut. Fig. 16. Calcite or alabaster bowl from Tarut.

by Rimush, and two inscribed by Naram-Sin, from Nippur, Ur, Tell Brak, Susa, and Drehem (Potts, n.d., Tables 1 and 2). In three cases, the Rimush vessels are labelled "booty of Elam". Potts has also suggested that a small alabaster sherd from Susa, labelled "booty of Magan" by Naram-Sin (cf. Potts 1986b:279), came from a vessel of the same type.

Fig. 17. Cylindrical alabaster vase from Tarut.

Thanks to the late M. Golding, we are fortunate in being able to publish yet another, more complete example of this vessel type from Tarut (Fig. 17). Apropos an Iranian origin for this type, as implied by the Elamite provenance of so many of Rimush's examples, one should note the presence of several very similar, if not identical, pieces at Shahdad (Hakemi 1972:Pl. XIIA and B, Pl. XIIIA). The form is also attested in Bactria as well (e.g. Pottier 1984:Pl. XXVI:207). A date between c. 2300 and 2100 B.C. is obviously implied by the presence of Sargonic royal inscriptions on a dozen vessels of this type.

A single, previously unpublished example of a shallow, *série récente* bowl is included here (Fig 18). It is decorated with an irregular row of drilled dots-in-double circle between two incised parallel lines. This particular form of decoration is already known from Tarut (viz. Zarins 1978:Pl. 71:565; Burkholder 1984:Pl. 19a; see Potts 1986a:151 for the catalogue numbers of *série récente* material in Zarins 1978). The product is surely of Omani origin, and finds very close parallels in finds from an Umm an-Nar period grave at Bat (Frifelt 1975:Fig. 28e); the surface of Bilad al-Maaidin (Weisgerber 1981:Abb. 43:3); and Maysar 1 (Weisgerber 1981:Abb. 46:5, 6 and 9). This suggests a date in the late third millennium, c. 2200-2000 B.C.

Fig. 18. *Série récente* soft-stone bowl from Tarut.

The link with the Umm an-Nar assemblages of the Oman peninsula suggested by the presence of substantial amounts of *série récente* finds on Tarut is further attested in the ceramic assemblage from the site. G. Burkholder reports that "many fine examples of Umm an Nar pottery" were found on Tarut, including a 19.5 cm. tall black-on-red jar with short neck and slightly everted rim which she has published (Burkholder 1984:190). This vessel finds a close parallel in several examples from Umm an-Nar island (Thorvildsen 1963:Fig. 21, middle right; Frifelt 1975:Fig. 10a; 1979:Fig. 2) and, with variations, in Tomb A at Hili North (Vogt 1985:Pl. 24:4). Fine ware of this sort is generally recognized as a typical component of Umm an-Nar funerary assemblages and is rare, although occasionally present in small quantities, in settlements (e.g. at Hili 8, see Cleuziou, n.d. Fig. 15:10, 16:15, and 20:5).

An additional example of black-on-red Umm an-Nar fineware from Tarut can now be added to the corpus (Fig. 19). As the photograph shows, the piece has been reconstructed from at least six sherds. It is broken at the neck but the shape is characteristic of Umm an-Nar vessels. The shoulder is decorated with a single zig-zag line between two parallel, concentric lines. Below this comes a broad metope of painted, overlapping chevrons, which is

Fig. 19. Black-on-red Umm an-Nar jar from Tarut.

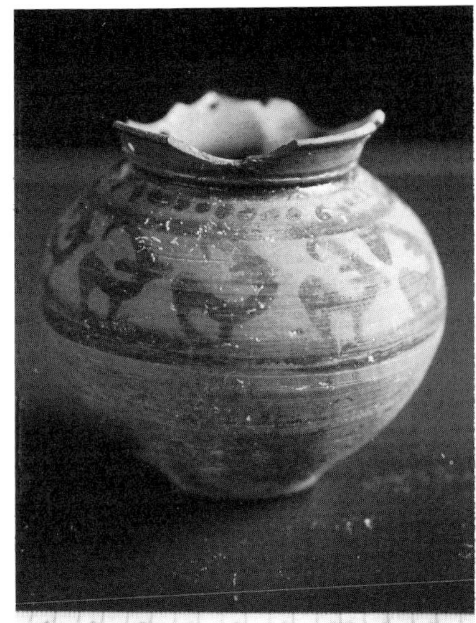

Fig. 20. Black-on-grey Umm an-Nar jar from Tarut.

bounded below by another pair of concentric parallel lines. The vessel can be paralleled generally with those examples cited above, and dates to the late third millennium. A close parallel for the zig-zagging line above a register of chevrons is found on a sherd from Amlah 1 (de Cardi, Collier and Doe 1976:Fig. 17:30).

Black-on-grey fineware is also known from Tarut (Anonymous 1975:148 center); Dhahran (Golding 1974:29); and Abqayq (Piesinger 1983:Fig. 61, Type 51). The Tarut exemplar, although previously published, is shown again here (Fig. 20) in a photograph which is superior to earlier ones. It is not certain that the vessel came from the main area of Tarut finds, however, for P. Arnot writes, "The statue <the nude male> and the gazelle pot are a puzzle" (Arnot 1986a). The Tarut vessel shows a number of drill holes below the rim, indicating that it was repaired in antiquity. The neck is decorated with a row of dots between two parallel, concentric lines. Below this, on the shoulder of the vessel, is a frieze of ibex standing on a base line. The piece has been illustrated recently in a popular work where, however, it is incorrectly said "to have been found near Abqaiq" (Rice 1985:244; the photograph there has also been printed back to front with the result that the caprids face left, whereas in fact they face right). Although the running ibex motif is more common on black-on-red canister jars, both in the Oman peninsula (e.g. Frifelt 1971:Fig. 2F [Umm an-Nar island]; Bibby 1967:Fig. 11 [great tomb at Hili]) and in Iran (de Cardi 1970:Fig. 43:481 [Bampur VI], cf. Fig. 37:108, 115 [Bampur V2]; Lamberg-Karlovsky and Tosi 1973:Fig. 64; Tosi 1976:Fig. 3; Tosi 1983:Fig. 8

Fig. 21. Copper or bronze bull's head from Tarut.

[Shahr-i Sokhta IV]), it is also attested on a squat, round-bellied jar with flaring rim, generally similar to the Tarut piece, from Tomb M at Hili (Cleuziou and Vogt 1985:Fig. 10). This latter vessel also shows the same band of dots beneath a line painted at the base of the neck, but differs from the Tarut exemplar in having three metopes of running caprids, rather than one. It is, moreover, like the canisters cited above, black-on-red and not black-on-grey. In this respect, the Tarut vessel is quite unusual. A strikingly similar depiction of the "silhouette of stylized ibex with long stressed horns, winding body, stressed ears and tail", virtually identical to that found on the Tarut vessel, is also known on painted buffware at Shahr-i Sokhta during periods II and III (Biscione and Bulgarelli 1983:235, motif 0145). The differences, however, between the ibexes shown on the Tarut vessel, and those which characterize the Bampur and Khurab assemblages, are indisputable (cf. Vanden Berghe 1955-56:30-31 for a systematic study of the painted motives in the pottery traditions of these two sites).

We come finally to the last object from Tarut of third millennium date which will be dealt with here, a hitherto unpublished copper or bronze bull's head (Fig. 21) acquired in 1967 from the former mayor (*'umdah*) of Qatif and now in a private collection. Whether the head came from the same mound as the other objects discussed here is unknown. Nor are any dimensions available for this important piece, but the camera lens cap beside it gives a rough indication of its small size. The present whereabouts of the object, said to have been acquired by a citizen of the U.K., are unknown to me.

Although the angle of the photograph makes it difficult to see the contour of the horns, these rise up from the head and curve inwards, although not excessively so. The head has no ears, but there seems to be a hole on the left side of the head, just below the horn, which might indicate that ears originally existed but have since been broken off. Stylistically the Tarut bull's head differs demonstrably from all of the Mesopotamian examples with which one is tempted to compare it, although these are in general more similar than the geographically closer yet stylistically aberrant bull's head from the Barbar temple on Bahrain (During Caspers 1971:Figs. 2-3). Unlike the many well-known bull's heads from the Royal Cemetery at Ur (e.g. Woolley 1934:Pl. 116 and 117 [U.12435], 119 [U.12351], 120 [U. 10577] or 143 [U.17887]), the Tarut head has narrow, slit-like eyes, instead of large round ones. Moreover, there are no folds above the eye, nor tufted hair between the horns. Although their eyes are round, the outline of the muzzle and nostrils on several stone sculptures from the Nintu temple at Khafajah and the Shara temple at Tell Agrab (Frankfort 1943:Pl. 51A-C, 52C-D) recalls that of the Tarut piece rather more than the Ur examples do.

Twenty years ago the late R.D. Barnett suggested that the bull's head from Bahrain may have come from a lyre like those used at Ur (Barnett 1969:101, n. 23). In this regard, it is important to stress the small size of the Tarut head, which makes it not unlikely that it served a similar function. One of Barnett's further observations concerned the discovery of copper strips, nails, a ring, and a band in the Barbar temple courtyard, which he thought may have come from the sound box of a lyre. It may not be irrelevant to note a further remark made by P. Arnot concerning the mound from which the bulk of the Tarut objects originated: "I did note in two places near the base of the mound single thin sheets of copper, badly deteriorated, over one foot <c. 30 cm.> in length. The copper material did not appear to have any significant thickness" (Arnot 1986a). It is tempting to speculate, as Barnett did, that the copper bull's head and the sheeting described here were the remains of a lyre, but in the present circumstance this possibility, if not unlikely, can never be verified. The copper sheeting from Tarut could, of course, date to an entirely different period.

In 1974 M. Golding published a greatly reduced drawing of a stamp seal of Persian Gulf type found at al-Khobar (Golding 1974:29). Here, we are able to publish photographs of its boss side (Fig. 22) and crudely incised face (Fig. 23). The al-Khobar seal, which appears to be made of serpentine or a similar green, veined stone, depicts a bull in profile, and a man with a club (?). The bull in profile is one of the most common iconographic elements on Persian Gulf seals (Potts, in press a), while the presence of a human in such cases is extremely rare. The date of this seal group is put c. 2100-1950 B.C. (Potts, in press b).

The region of al-Hasa enjoyed a certain degree of prosperity during the third millennium, when it was manifestly linked both with southern Iran and

Fig. 22. Obverse of a Persian Gulf seal from al-Khobar.

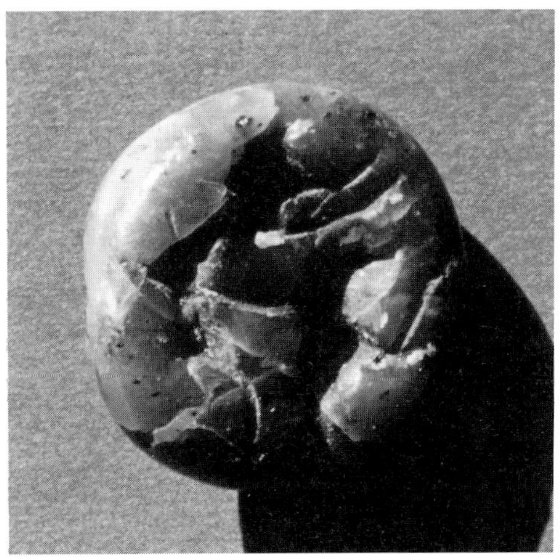

Fig. 23. Reverse of a Persian Gulf seal from al-Khobar.

the Oman peninsula to the south, and Mesopotamia to the north. The rich and varied finds from Tarut in particular reflect the presence of an affluent community there. Unfortunately, the quarrying of the mound at al-Rufayah has destroyed for all time what was obviously an important site. The nature of the site is thus difficult to ascertain. Was it a cemetery? The only clearly observed graves in the mound, the cist graves, are much younger and should be kept out of the discussion here. On the other hand, the recovery of complete or nearly complete Umm an-Nar type ceramic vessels, as well as stone vessels with parallels in, for example, the Jamdat Nasr cemetery at Ur, does suggest that there were some third millennium graves here. At the same time it should not be forgotten that temples are the most common findspot of *série ancienne* steatite vessels in Mesopotamia (items such as the bull's head and the nude male statue cannot be attributed to the al-Rufayah mound with complete certainty, and thus should be ignored for present purposes). It would not be difficult to imagine the existence of a third millennium temple at al-Rufayah which, having been mounded over by time of the Seleucid-Parthian period, was then used as a cemetery into which plaster-lined cist graves were set.

That there was a temple or substantial public building on Tarut in the near vicinity is suggested by P. Arnot's description of dressed limestone masonry on the island: "The road from the old fort area <Tarut town> eastward to the burial mound crosses by a crude bridge over a rather deep irrigation ditch. My memory is rather vague but I guess that the bridge was about one hundred or more yards <+ 100 m.> from the fort. A portion of the west wall of the irrigation ditch exposed a section of a wall constructed of dressed limestone blocks. The face of the block was about two by two feet <c. 60 x 60 cm.>. These nicely dressed blocks almost had to be part of an ancient structure of some importance. (I am reasonably sure a date grower did not haul in these blocks to line the ditch)....(Bibby and others did locate an old limestone quarry west of Jubail)" (Arnot 1986a). Surely the quality of the Tarut finds makes it entirely conceivable that at least one major third millennium building was located on the island. T.G. Bibby has suggested that the limestone masonry protruding from the face of the tell in the center of Tarut town might represent "a citadel, a palace or a temple...as the focal point of a wider settlement of the island" (Bibby 1973:31). Pending eventual investigation of these remains and those described by Arnot (if they still exist), however, we would prefer not to assume a third millennium date for either site. One should not assume, on analogy with the Barbar temples, that all buildings of cut limestone in this general vicinity must date to the Bronze Age. As is well known, the urban site of Thaj, which dates to the Seleucid and Parthian periods, was built entirely of cut limestone masonry. The Tarut tell or the remains observed in the irrigation ditch could date just as easily to third century as to the third millennium. Indeed, this was the tentative conclusion of A.H. Masry who, in 1972, dug a 2 x 4 m. sondage "along the lower-middle slopes of the exposed western side of the mound", and found that "Levels 5 and 6 were associated with massive masonry wall structures...(which) apparently belong to the Seleucid period" (Masry 1974:143).

The Second Millennium

CHAPTER II

Very little material from northeastern Arabia can, at present, be attributed to the second millennium B.C. As this has been reviewed elsewhere (Potts, in press a and b), we will only recapitulate here in brief what is already known. Red-ridged pottery of City II type, well-known on Bahrain, has been found all along the coast from Dhahran to Jubayl, suggesting that ties with Bahrain were strong in the early centuries of the millennium. This view is supported, moreover, by the fact that Dilmun sac-shaped burial jars have been found in the Dhahran Airport mound field, while at least three Dilmun seals are known from al-Hasa as well. Links with Iran may be indicated by parallels in the Dhahran Airport burial corpus to pottery belonging to the Kaftari tradition in Fars. On the other hand, ties to the Oman peninsula did not cease altogether at the end of the third millennium. A socketed bronze spearhead from a grave in the Yabrin oasis points clearly to the Wadi Suq assemblages in Oman and the U.A.E. Similarly, both the Dhahran graves and the Tarut corpus from al-Rufayah contain unequivocal examples of *série tardive*, second millennium steatite vessels. With regard to northern ties, a series of flat and ring-based goblets of Kassite and/or Middle Elamite affinity is now known from a tomb in the Dhahran Airport site (Zarins, Mughannum and Kamal 1984:Pl. 43, Tomb A6).

It is therefore of some interest to present here a small number of bronze arrowheads which may be dated to the second millennium and thus provide a further link with the Wadi Suq assemblages of the Oman peninsula. The most interesting piece is an inscribed, lanceolate arrowhead (Fig. 24) from the surface of a site near Jabal Kenzan (see Fig. 1). This site has been described by G. Burkholder (Burkholder 1984:35-38). It is a sandy area with a multitude of visible burial mounds; open gravel pans with a surface scatter of artifacts; the remains of relict lake beds; and the scattered remains of buildings. A prominent red *jabal* is the most visible landmark in the area, rising about 7 m. above the surrounding plain. The surfaces of the broad, central midrib on the Jabal Kenzan arrowhead are flat, and the "inscription" consists of an X between two short, horizontal strokes. No fewer than eighteen arrowheads of this type were found in a Wadi Suq period long grave, SH 102, at Shimal in northern Ras al-Khaimah (Vogt and Franke-Vogt 1987:Figs. 19-20). Similar examples are also known from a Wadi Suq grave excavated at Ghalilah (Donaldson 1984:Fig. 26:6-9) and from the so-called "Mound of Serpents" at al-Qusais (Lombard 1985:208, Fig. 105:364; for the site, see Taha 1982-83).

Although this type of arrowhead had formerly been dated to the Iron Age (e.g. Lombard 1985:208; Phillips 1987:15 and Fig. 38), B. Vogt argues convincingly that it is a second millennium leitfossil which is intrusive when it appears in later Iron Age contexts. He points, for instance, to the occurrence of a similar arrowhead in a grave at Hassan Zamini, in the Iranian Talish, which also contained a cylinder seal in the Mitanni Common Style (H. de Morgan 1905:Fig. 543), and to less clearly related, but incised, arrowheads from Tell al-'Ajjul in Palestine of MB IIB or LB I date (Vogt and Franke-Vogt 1987:35).

Uninscribed arrowheads, similar in shape to those under discussion, have also been found in 15th-14th century contexts at both Nuzi (Starr 1937:Pl. 125:P, W, JJ) and Tell Zubeidi (Boehmer and Dämmer 1985:Taf. 150:667, 670). To these may be added at least one more from Jabal Kenzan (Fig. 25, second from left), and two (Fig. 26, left and center) from the Dhahran-Dammam-Al-Khobar area. One of these (Fig. 26 center) is of the broad, foliate variety, which also finds close parallels with inscribed examples from SH 102 (Vogt and Franke-Vogt 1987:Fig. 20:9) and uninscribed pieces from al-Qusais (Lombard 1985:Fig. 105:353-354). The condition of the remainder of the arrowheads shown on these figures (Fig. 27) is too poor to admit closer dating.

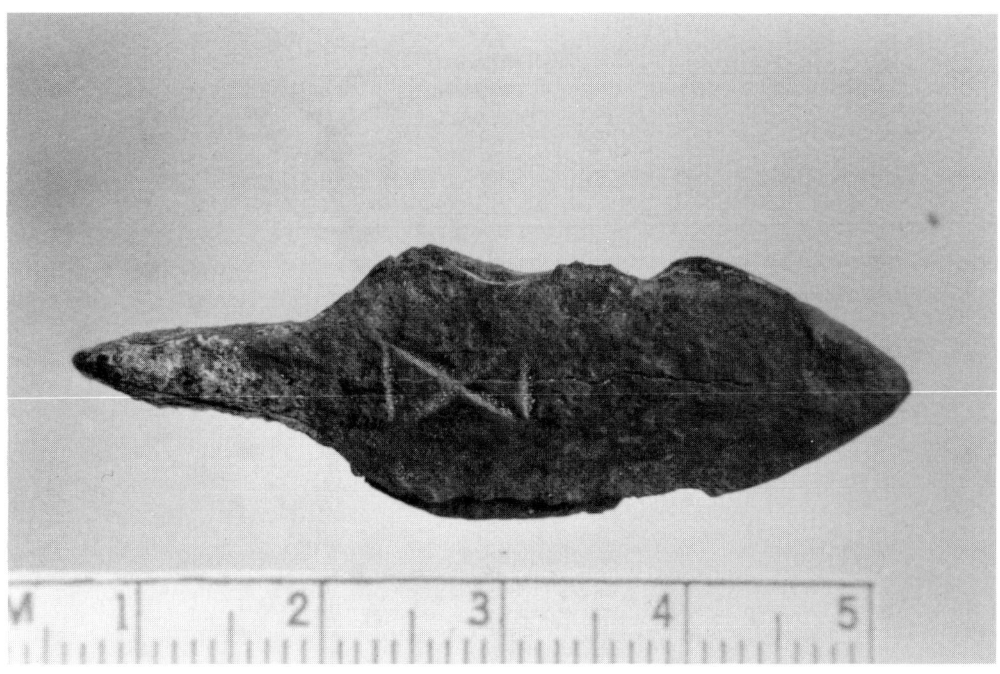

Fig. 24. Inscribed lanceolate bronze arrowhead from Jabal Kenzan.

Fig. 25. Bronze arrowheads from Jabal Kenzan.

Fig. 26. Bronze arrowheads from the Dhahran-Dammam-al-Khobar area.

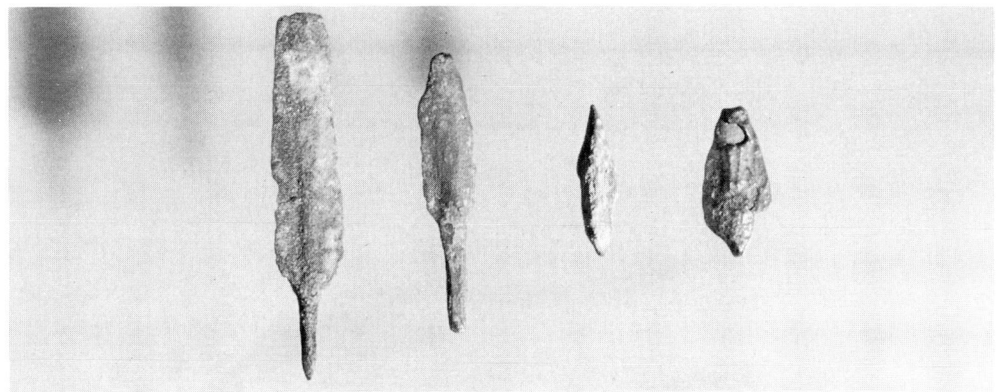

Fig. 27. Bronze arrowheads from the Dhahran-Dammam-al-Khobar area.

Fig. 28. Impression of a fragmentary cylinder seal from the Salt Mine site.

Fig. 29. Impression of a cylinder seal from the Salt Mine site.

The Iron Age

CHAPTER III

There is little doubt that the Iron Age is the least well-documented period in the archaeological sequence of al-Hasa. In the Oman peninsula, a rich and varied Iron Age culture is represented at sites like Rumeilah (Boucharlat and Lombard 1985), Hili 2, Fashgha 1 (Phillips 1987), and Lizq (see Lombard 1985 for a recent synthesis of the material; cf. Potts, in press a). On Bahrain, a large building complex with Neo-Assyrian and Neo-Babylonian affinities was excavated at Qalat al-Bahrain by the Danish expedition (Oates 1986, Lombard 1986). The mainland, however, has not yielded much material of Iron Age date, and what little is known comes principally from the Salt Mine site, between Hofuf and al-Uqayr.

In a recent study of the Salt Mine site, P. Lombard has treated a small group of cylinder seals which show Neo-Assyrian, Neo-Babylonian, or Achaemenid characteristics (Lombard 1988:Figs. 8-11). Two of these seals will be briefly re-examined here. The first (Fig. 28), of unknown material, is badly preserved, as the sloppily made seal impression shows, and was left unillustrated by Lombard. Nevertheless, the bodies of two quadrupeds can be made out. Their legs are clear, ending in feet shaped like dots. The left figure (center of the photograph) appears to have wings emanating from its right shoulder, and this trait, combined with the peculiar, drilled rendering of the feet, remind one of the depiction of animals on several cylinder seals in the Neo-Assyrian Linear Style (Buchanan 1966:Pl. 41:620-621; cf. Von der Osten 1934:Pl. XXIX:436 and, for the carving technique, Pl. XXX:440), and perhaps more so in the Neo-Assyrian Drilled Style (e.g. Porada 1948:Pl. CII, 690E, Pl. CVI, 716, Pl. CVII, 723). As B. Buchanan noted, however, speaking of Neo-Assyrian glyptic, seals "with a simplified treatment of animal form had a wide distribution and perhaps a long range in time" (Buchanan 1966:106).

The second seal shown here (Fig. 29, cf. Lombard 1988:Fig. 11) shows a skirted figure facing left. In its left hand it holds a mace or torch (?) from which four lines (flames?) emanate. Its right hand grasps a staff which seems to rise up from a mountain-like feature. To its right is a second skirted figure, facing right, its left arm stretched out and down behind it, its right hand grasping a staff, the top of which terminates in a round ball or mace-head. Both figures seem to wear hats or have an elevated coiffure, although these are not at all clear in the photograph. To the right is a crouching dog with short, curved tail. Above this is a large, roughly triangular or inverted pear-shaped face, the eyes, nose, and mouth of which are clear. Two lines frame it on either side (hair?). Two stick-like limbs, ending in claws like chicken feet, project downward from the sides of the face. Above it is an area of contiguous curving lines which recall an early glyptic convention for depicting mountains. The scene is bounded on both the top and bottom by a hatched border.

Lombard noted that, while the border suggested a first millennium B.C. date, the "puzzling iconography" made it not unlikely that this seal is a forgery (Lombard 1988). R.M. Boehmer, to whom I showed a photograph of this piece, expressed the opinion that, had it come from a traditional seal-using area, it would undoubtedly be pronounced a forgery, but as it was found in eastern Arabia one must keep an open mind and be ready to accept unorthodox iconography which does not conform to the established practices of glyptic decoration. Moreover, as we both agreed, the likelihood of a cylinder seal having been forged in this area, where no antiquities market *per se* existed, and the fact that the seal was specifically said to come from the Salt Mine site, and was photographed along with other objects which came from the site, makes it unwise to reject it as unauthentic. In the present circumstances, I will assume that the seal is genuine.

In an effort to clarify both the date and affiliation of this seal, I would like to shift the focus away from a search for links to Assyrian and Babylonian glyptic, and consider instead the peculiarly un-Mesopotamian frontal, flat, triangular face. This seemingly bizarre representation is in fact well-attested in northwestern Arabia in various media during the course of at least five centuries. A similar, if more perfectly triangular face, with two eyes and straight lines for the nose and mouth, is engraved on the surface of a boulder at Jabal Ghunaym, southeast of Tayma (Anonymous 1975:81 bottom; Winnett and Reed 1970:Fig. 36). The presence there of a large group of what F.V. Winnett has termed Taymanite inscriptions containing dedications to the Arabian deity Salm (Winnett and Reed 1970:93-108; cf. Roschinski 1981:51) originally led H.St.J.B. Philby to identify this figure with Salm, and in this Winnett and Reed concur, dating the image to the sixth century, when Salm was worshipped at Tayma (see most recently Dalley 1986:85-86), as the famous Tayma stone reveals (Winnett and Reed 1970:29, 34). The same face occurs, moreover, among another group of Taymanite texts mentioning Salm at the site of Mantar Bani ʻAtiya (Parr, Harding and Dayton 1972:Fig. 8), a watch tower located some eight kilometers northwest of Tayma. Much later, however, the frontal face without the triangular shape is found, for example, on dedicatory stelae from Petra (Hammond 1981:139; cf. Baratte and Zayadine 1987:213-215), while in southern Arabia numerous examples are known (e.g. from Hajar Bin Humeid, see Van Beek 1969:271, Fig. 116g; cf. Cleveland 1965:Pls. 37-39, from Timna; Rathjens and Von Wissmann 1932:Phot. 150-152, provenance unknown; Pirenne 1977:I.551, 553, both in the British Museum).

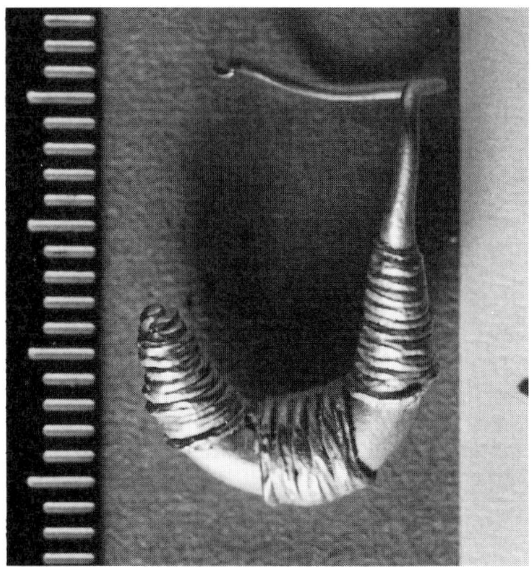

Fig. 30. Gold earring from the Salt Mine site.

In view of the peculiarly Arabian significance of the frontal, triangular face with stylized eyes, nose, and mouth, I would not hesitate to confirm the authenticity of the Salt Mine site seal, and would be tempted to suggest an origin during the Neo-Babylonian or early Achaemenid period in northwestern Arabia. Might we be in the presence of a Taymanite cylinder seal?

We turn now to a gold earring from the Salt Mine Site (Fig. 30). The earring consists of a crescent with three areas of ribbing which have been formed by winding gold wire around the terminus, middle, and upper body of the crescent. Although the date is difficult to determine, good parallels exist for just this type of earring in Late Assyrian graves at Assur (Haller 1954:Taf. 20a, 37d; cf. Maxwell-Hyslop 1971:238 and Figs. 129-130, her "Type I, Crescent-shaped earrings"). Perhaps not unrelated are the plain, boat-shaped earrings (slightly thicker in the body than the crescent-shaped ones) from War Kabud in Luristan (late 8th/7th century B.C.) and the more elaborate ones, decorated with granulation, from Tumulus A at Gordion (Maxwell-Hyslop 1971:Pls. 250, 247). At Ur, a hoard of jewellery found "under the Persian and above the Nebuchadnezzar pavement in room 5 of E-nun-mah" contained gold earrings of similar shape, but with different applied decoration (Woolley 1962:Pl. 22, U.460A, B, 461, 462, 464). Several of these were plain crescents, with no gold wire added; others have various patterns of granulation and wire wrapped around the terminus and upper body. A completely plain crescent was also recovered from an Achaemenid copper coffin (Woolley 1962:Pl. 24, U.6677). This type of earring, generally speaking, seems to have been Syrian in origin, and to have gone out of fashion by the mid-fourth century B.C. (Kraay and Moorey 1969:195-196).

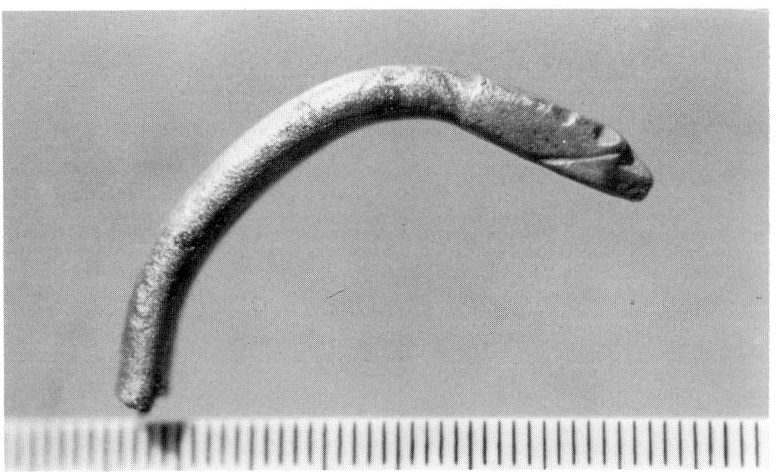

Fig. 31. Fragment of a gold snake bracelet from the Dhahran-Dammam-al-Khobar area.

The final object of Iron Age date which we shall consider here is a fragment of a cast gold bracelet with a finial in the form of a snake's head from the Dhahran-Dammam-al-Khobar area (Fig. 31). It is difficult to be certain of the date of this object, but several clues point to the Iron Age, whether early or late. Despite the superficial similarity of this piece to a snake headed scepter from Susa (J. De Morgan 1905:47, Fig. 70, and Pl. XVII:1; cf. Grohmann 1914:73, Abb. 194), this comparison must be ruled out because of the difference in size of these two objects. "Bracelets with serpents' heads", however, formed a genre of Iron Age jewellery in the Urartian realm, and these are represented in Iran as well (Maxwell-Hyslop 1971:205 and Pl. 162). In general, of course, bracelets terminating in finials in the form of animals' heads are well-known in this part of the world in both pre-Achaemenid, Achaemenid, and Seleucid contexts, and a delicate pair of gold bracelets with finials in the form of bulls' calves, thought to come from Ziwiye, resembles the present piece (cf. Maxwell-Hyslop 1971:Pl. 171b). A similar bracelet of bronze, the animal finials of which are difficult to identify, was found in a grave dated to the late fifth century B.C. at Ras Shamra/Leukos Limen (Stucky 1983:87-88, Taf. 31:21). Less similar is a pair of silver bracelets with snake-headed finials from Tall-i Takht which, on the basis of associated coins, are dated to c. 280 B.C. (Stronach 1978:178, Fig. 90:1-2). It is thus in the context of pieces such as these that we would situate this surface find from the Dhahran-Dammam region.

The Seleucid and Parthian Periods

CHAPTER IV

During the Seleucid and Parthian periods, settlement flourished all over al-Hasa, from Hofuf to Jubayl. The great metropolis of the period was Thaj (cf. Mandaville 1963; Bibby 1973:10-27; Potts 1984:102-105; in press a), a large walled city located c. 90 km. west of Jubayl along a track known as the Darb al-Kunhuri. As the only site of such proportions in northeastern Arabia, and one on which the ruins of stone architecture are everywhere visible on the surface, Thaj has always been a favorite spot for outings by members of the ARAMCO community with an interest in archaeology. It is to them that we owe the discovery of a number of interesting surface finds which will be presented here.

Thaj

We begin with a pair of bronze stamp seals. Hitherto, no seals from Thaj have been published, and indeed seals, engraved gems, and cameos are rare in the Gulf region during the Seleucid and Parthian periods. The first example (Figs. 32-34) is round, with a flat, oval boss. Although it appears to be made of stone in the photographs, its owner states that it is made of bronze. The face shows a winged quadruped, the tail, wings, and forelegs of which are clear. The head is indistinct, making identification difficult, but the whole aspect of the beast is that of a winged horse, an animal frequently depicted on oval seals used to seal both bullae (e.g. Amiet 1957:Pl. XX:114,1) and tablets (e.g. Speleers 1917:230-233, nos. 197, 198, and 201 from Warka) in Seleucid Mesopotamia. Less similar but no doubt iconographically related are an engraved bronze plaque of Seleucid date from the Great Temple at Masjid-i Solaiman showing Pegasus (Ghirshman 1976:88, Pl. XCVIII:1), and a stamp seal of chalcedony showing a winged horse above a fish which H.H. von der Osten called Greco-Persian (Von der Osten 1957:144, no. 203). The Thaj seal also shows an important symbol engraved beneath the winged horse, namely the symbol of Seleucid royal power, the anchor (cf. generally McDowell 1935:31, 33). Here, for reasons of space, the anchor is shown horizontally, with the cross-bar to the right, and its curving hooks to the left. Introduced as a symbol by Seleucus I on his coinage while still one of Alexander's satraps, the anchor was adopted as a royal symbol by the kings of Elymais, who used it not only on monetary issues but even show it on some of their crowns (von Gall

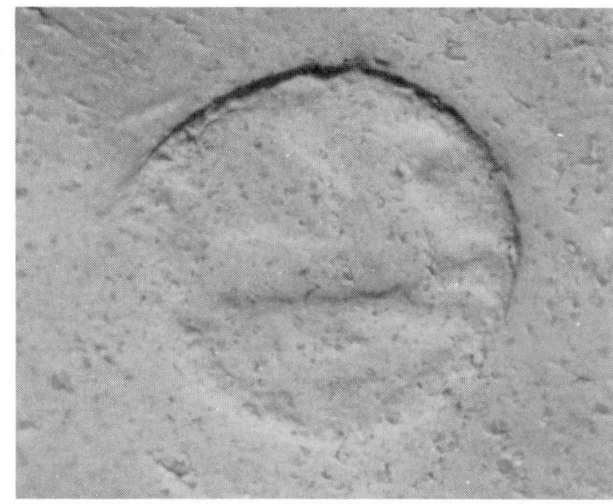

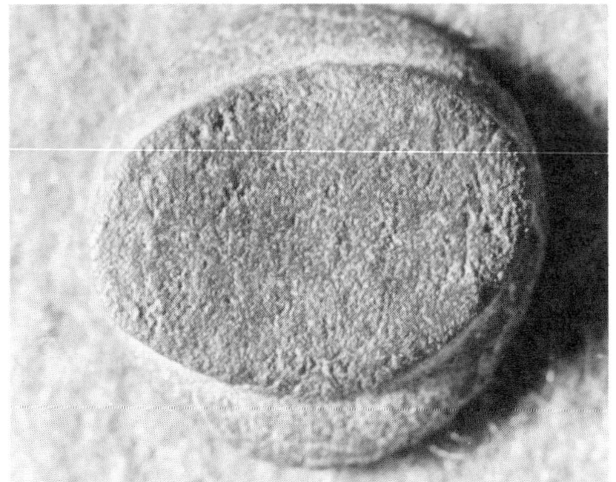

Figs. 32-34. Bronze stamp seal and impression from Thaj.

1980:246-250). The Thaj seal thus combines a winged horse, a favorite subject of Hellenistic artisans, with the anchor, a royal symbol of the house of Seleucus.

The second seal (Figs. 35-37) from Thaj is a flat, bronze, irregular ovoid disc. In form it resembles the bezel of a seal-ring (cf. Vollenweider 1983:No. 65, of Achaemenid date), but as the photograph of the unengraved side shows, it was never attached to anything else and it seems unlikely that a jeweller would make and engrave a bezel apart from an entire ring. The engraving is poor and the head is all but obliterated, but nevertheless a prancing, short-tailed quadruped can easily be discerned. In its general attitude, the animal resembles a horse, but for the two deeply etched strokes above the head which give it the appearance of a long-eared ass or donkey. Numerous examples of long-horned goats and rams are known on engraved Greek gems (e.g. Vollenweider 1967:no. 210, 1983:no. 212) and on Achaemenid stamp seals (e.g. Von der Osten 1936:Pl. XII:134), but the straightness of the appendages shown here differs markedly from such representations. A four sided, rectangular stamp seal from Susa, however, may give a clue to the intepretation of the animal. There a long-eared hare is shown in almost exactly the same posture

Figs. 35-37. Bronze stamp seal and impression from Thaj.

(Delaporte 1920:Pl. 54:33d, D.137).

Over the years a large number of figurine fragments have been found on the surface of Thaj. By far the most common are female (e.g. Bibby 1969:327; Burkholder 1984:Pl. 48) and camel figurines (e.g. Burkholder 1984:Pl. 46b). P. Arnot writes, "These figurines were concentrated (lots of them and probably almost (?) all gleaned by Aramco pot pickers) at Thaj" (Arnot 1986b). Elsewhere, they seem to be rare in northeastern Arabia. Bowen published the body and head of a pair of camel figurines from the surface of Ayn Jawan (Bowen 1950:Fig. 21), and P. Arnot reports that, "The Thaj pottery figurines were found in limited numbers in the area northwest of Al Khobar. I personally found two of the camel figures and others reported finding the woman figurine" (Arnot 1986b); "You would have expected to have found some at Jubail but we really combed that area (a very popular pot picking area) and we never found a figurine nor did I hear of any one finding one. Therefore, I had to conclude that the figurine people had to have resided only at Thaj with figurines of busty women and camels with harness" (Arnot 1986b). At least one example of a Thaj-type female figurine is, however, also known from Bahrain (on display in the National Museum).

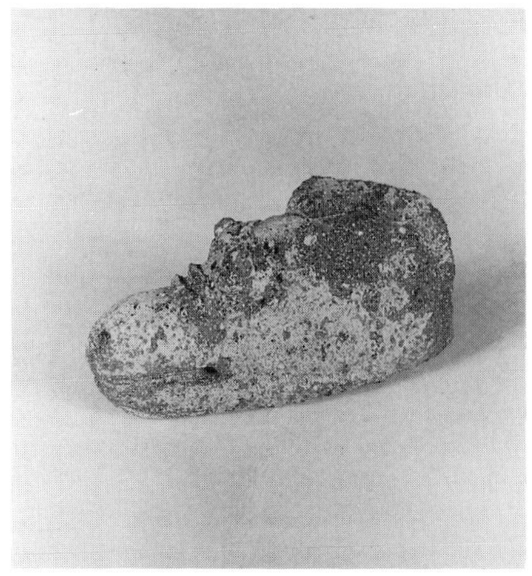

Figs. 38-39. Head of a terracotta camel figurine from Thaj.

We include here only a single representative of the camel group (Figs. 38-39). Like much of the indigenous pottery from Thaj, the camel head is made of a gritty red clay, so fired that an irregular white surface has appeared. The features of the camel, including its mouth, nose, snout folds, and eyes were incised or modelled before firing. In addition, a ring of punctations encircles each eye. Attention should be drawn here to the tradition of manufacturing cast bronze camel figurines in Southern Arabia (e.g. Grohmann 1927:174, Abb. 73; Rathjens and Von Wissmann 1932:Phot. 163)

A recently published, complete example of a Thaj female figurine (Anonymous 1983:Pl. 99) gives an excellent impression of how the many body fragments found all over the site should be interpreted. The figure is nude. It is shown seated, as if on a throne or stool, inclining slightly backwards. The legs are large, and the pubic area, outlined by an incised triangle, is decorated with small punctations. The arms are bent at the elbow, with the forearms flat against the chest. On analogy with other Oriental female figurines, it appears as if the figure were cupping her breasts in her two hands. The neck is shown as a series of modelled folds. The head is schematic, and the nose has been pinched. The eyes are crudely incised, and the figure's hair is shown in braids hanging down to its neck. In view of the fact that we know virtually nothing of the indigenous religion of this region during the Seleucid era, it would be rash to interpret this as a "mother goddess", and try to identify it with a member of the pre-Islamic Arabian pantheon. Rather, we will concentrate on the stylistic analysis of the fragments shown here.

We begin with the head of a figurine (Fig. 40). In comparison with many known examples (e.g. Burkholder 1984:Pl. 48), this is an elaborate and realistic representation. Considerable attention has been paid to the eyes, which are not mere pin-pricks in the clay, but have appliqué eyelids and eyeballs.

Fig. 40. Head of a terracotta female figurine from Thaj.

The hair shows a row of small punctations at the right brow, curls running down the right side, and short hatch marks on the left. Three neck folds are visible. Unfortunately, neither the nose nor the mouth is preserved.

In comparison with this example, the next piece (Figs. 41-43) has a much more schematic head. Here, there is no distinction between the neck and head. The elongation above the shoulders is dotted at the neck, as if to indicate a necklace (cf. the same convention on South Arabian sculpture from Timna, Cleveland 1965:Pl. 51, TC 2530), and a double row of dots runs across the chest. A nose has been pinched out of this piece of clay, resembling a bird's beak, and an eye is indicated on the left side with a small globule of

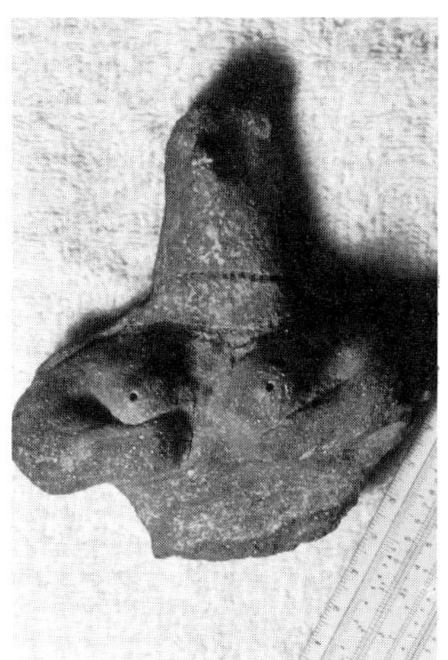

Figs. 41-43. Bust of a terracotta female figurine from Thaj.

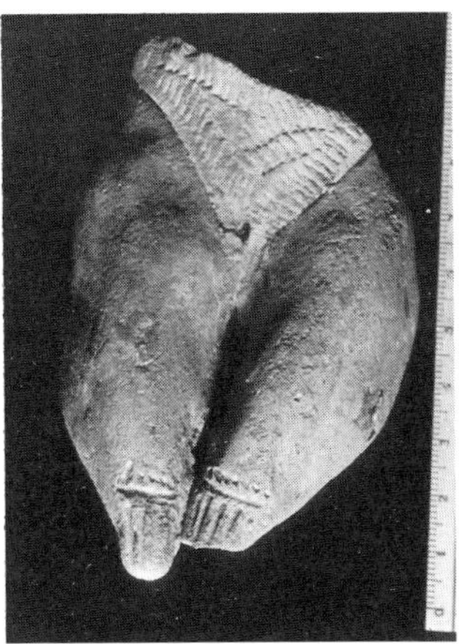

Fig. 44. Legs of a terracotta female figurine from Thaj.

Figs. 45-46 (below). Torso of a terracotta male (?) figurin from Thaj.

clay. A ridge of clay on either side of the head suffices to denote the long, flowing tresses of the figure, whose hands are cupped under each breast. A long ridge running down the back of the figure's neck may be meant to indicate a single braid.

The lower half of a typical female figurine (Fig. 44) shows a heavily incised, pubic area; large, crudely modelled legs; and curious dots and strokes to indicate the feet.

Although male figurines from Thaj have not received much attention, the next example shown here (Figs. 44-46) lacks the typical female attributes of the other figurines discussed. While the available photographs are not particularly clear, there are no breasts visible and no pubic triangle. Instead, the navel of the figure is accentuated by a ring of small dots. The posture of the figure recalls that of the complete figurine found on the surface of Thaj in

Fig. 47. Torso of a terracotta male (?) figurine from Thaj.

Figs. 48-49 (below). Rump of a stone animal figurine.

1983 (Anonymous 1983:Pl. 99), reclining slightly to the rear. The eyes and nostrils are shown by deep punctations, while the mouth is shown as a short stroke. The arms, although broken, are bent at the elbow and seem to be shown held in front of the chest.

Another fragment of a male figurine is also illustrated here (Fig. 47). Although the head, arms, and legs are largely missing, it is clear that the groin of the figure is completely different from that of the Thaj female figurines. A large navel, with a raised round knob of clay ringed by small dots, is shown above what appears to be the figure's genitals, also ringed by dots.

To the clay figurines of Thaj can be added a unique fragment (Figs. 48-49) of limestone, showing the rear of an animal, unfortunately broken off at the haunches. The animal's short tail is particularly clear.

Figs. 50-51. South Arabian scaraboid stamp seal from the Salt Mine site.

The Salt Mine Site

We have already spoken of the Salt Mine site in connection with finds made there of Iron Age date. The site is also the source of two engraved gems and two seals which we present here. The first seal (Fig. 50-51) is a scaraboid, South Arabian stamp seal. The oval field is ringed by a line and divided into three registers by two horizontal lines. Between these we see a kneeling hero grappling with a rearing quadruped, the hatched mane of which makes it look like a lion. Below the scene is something that looks like a fish. Above the scene is a fragmentary and barely visible legend written in South Arabian letters. Scaraboid stamp seals are well-known in Southern Arabia (Grohmann 1914:46, Abb. 111, and 1927:176; Caton Thompson 1944:Pl. XLIV:9), and the convention of dividing the field into three registers is attested there as well (e.g. Pirenne 1977:I.598, Berlin Museum no. 2622). The iconography of the seal is extremely interesting, and belies Greco-Roman influence. If the animal shown is a lion, then the scene may well be Heracles slaying the Nemean lion. If it is a horse, which seems less likely from the animal's proportions but cannot be ruled out altogether, then the scene may be that of Heracles subduing one of the horses of Diomedes (cf. Harle 1985). In the present instance, we would opt for the first possibility however, and assume that the seal was manufactured in Southern Arabia, whence it reached al-Hasa sometime during the Hellenistic period.

Fig. 52. South Arabian stamp seal from the Salt Mine site.

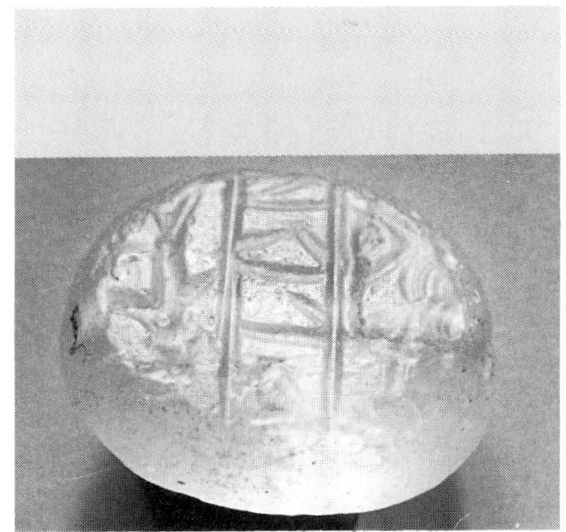

Fig. 53 lower left. Engraved gem from the Salt Mine site.

Fig. 54 lower right. Engraved gem from the Salt Mine site.

A second stamp seal from the Salt Mine site is very poorly preserved (Fig. 52) but may also be classified as South Arabian. Once again, we see two horizontal lines dividing the field into three registers. In this case, there appears to be a fish (?) in the lowest register. Fragments of a South Arabian legend can be made out in the middle register (cf. Turner 1973:Pl. XLVIII:A for a South Arabian seal divided into four registers with recumbent gazelle in both the top and bottom register).

Finally, we have two engraved gems (Figs. 53-54) from the Salt Mine site, both of which show leaping quadrupeds, a subject which is by no means un-

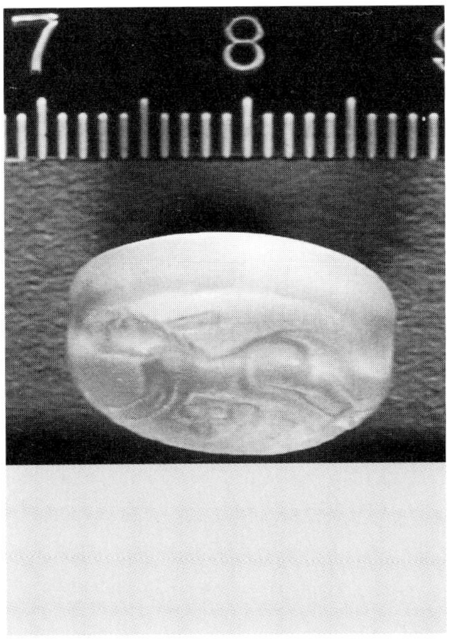

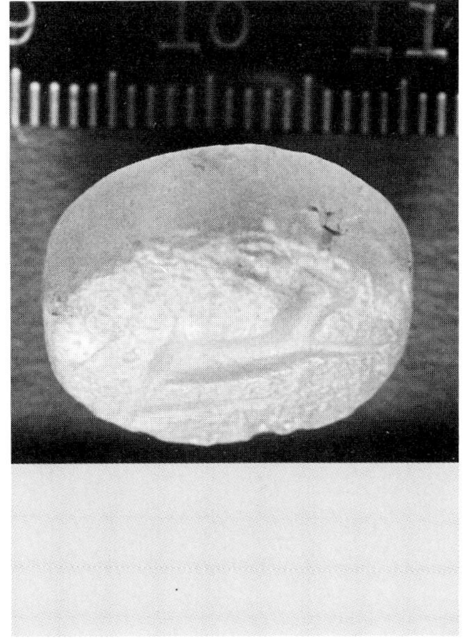

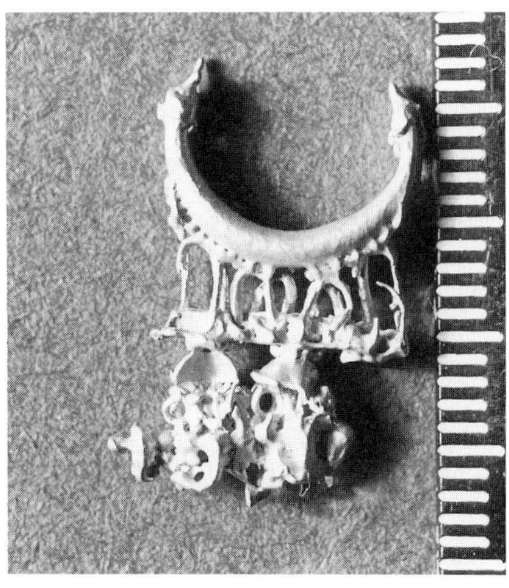

Fig. 55. Gold earring from the Salt Mine site.

common on Greek gems (e.g. Vollenweider 1967:Pl. 80:5, 10, 11, 81:1-8). In one case (Fig. 53) the mane and long tail suggest that the animal may be a horse; in the second, more schematized seal (Fig. 54), the horn and short, upright tail recall something more akin to a gazelle. It is difficult to determine whether these are crude Greek gems or whether they belong in the category of Greco-Persian gems (cf. Von der Osten 1936:Pl. XII, no. 134), but the quality of the engraving perhaps argues for the latter possibility.

The last object from the Salt Mine site to be presented here is a gold earring (Fig. 55), previously published by E. Porada (Porada 1967:106, Pl. XXIV:4a-b). The earring consists of a pendant crescent, from which a net of fine gold strands hangs. These, in turn, support a pair of bells. Porada dated the earring to the fourth century because of the presence of a tetradrachm of Alexander minted at Byblos c. 320-315 B.C. which was found in the vicinity (Lombard 1988:Fig. 6a-b). In fact, as we have seen, objects of different date have been recovered from the site, and thus the earring should not be dated by the stray coin. Nevertheless, the affinities of this piece to Hellenistic jewellery, as shown by Porada, are clear.

Tarut

As noted in Chapter I, not all the finds from the mound on Tarut were of third millennium date. Some of these come from cist graves which had been built into the mound, and which produced a group of finds attributable to the Seleucid or Parthian era. P. Arnot (1986a) described the general situation as follows:

"I was with the Goldings and others on one visit. The top material of the mound that was being mined was sufficiently firm to leave a vertical face. Several caskets (coffins) <plaster-lined cists> with their broken ends were exposed from the face of the mound. The caskets appeared to have been cast using a white cement like material (probably from a crude burnt gypsum cement - plaster of Paris - which was still being made in Qatif in my time). The Goldings were able to recover a couple of alabaster bowls from one of the exposed broken caskets. I noted only three of the cast caskets in <the> entire face of the mound. Therefore, I speculate that the casket usage was limited to the more affluent burials.

There were numerous crude headstone markers in the debris. The markers were about six inches in diameter and about eighteen inches in length made from crude casting of local cemented coarse aggregate or more likely carved from sea rock - furish <farush>. The markers were about the same size and material as the ones that were photographed except that <they> did not have the carved head and pin base. Markings were not found on these stones.

The mound face exposed a remarkable number of small bowls of poor quality pottery. The bowls were not stratified in the face but scattered throughout in a random fashion. I noted at least four bowls in a clump at one spot - not nested. The photos include a picture of five of these bowls and Vidal <F.S. Vidal, former ARAMCO anthropologist> expressed an opinion that they were 'lids', and one picture shows where he placed one of the small bowls on a beaker to demonstrate his lid theory. This 'lid' theory must have been passed on to Bibby as he comments as follows: '--the five lids (which I think are lamps)'. The present of the great number of the small bowls in the mound was suggestive (to an amateur) that they were votive cups....

On my last visit to the mound, I noticed an area about two hundred feet <c. 60 m.> east nearer to the coast that the locals had very recently dug a pattern of shallow ditches, probably for a garden project. The area was not a mound. The ditches had cut through an old burial ground where the remains had been interred in pots. The ditches had cut through the pots exposing a lot of bones. I made no attempt to recover a complete pot. The pots did appear to be about two feet plus <+60 cm.> in height, pot bellied and at least one foot <c. 30 cm.> in diameter."

These precious descriptions contain a wealth of information. The account of the plaster-lined cists immediately recalls a number of graves of Parthian date west of Jidd Hafs, south of the Budaiya road, and close to Sar, excavated by the Danish expedition in 1954, 1959, and 1960 (Bibby 1954:138-141; Glob 1959:238, 1960:212). Ten similarly constructed cist graves "all built into one irregularly shaped mound" were also investigated by Capt. Higham "2 to 3 kms.

Figs. 56-57. Obverse and reverse sides of a stone grave stela from Tarut.

east of the Portuguese fort" during the 1960's (During Caspers 1972-74:148-156). More recently, both cist graves and jar burials have been excavated at Janussan by a French mission (Lombard and Salles 1984; Salles 1986).

Thankfully, the "headstone markers" described by Arnot were among the objects photographed on Tarut in 1966. One has already been published (Burkholder 1984:Pl. 37), and two more are included here. The first (Figs. 56-57) is approximately 40 cm. tall, fairly crude, and apparently built of farush or local beach-rock. It is in fact a small stela with a semi-round head set on a semi-cylindrical body of slightly larger diameter, the whole resting on a smaller peg. The back side of the stela is roughly flat. The second example (Fig. 58) is known only from a photograph taken from behind, but it shows clearly that the peg of the stela was meant to stand in a roughly rectangular stone base. The second example appears better made than the first. The smoothing of the backside is more accomplished, and the "shoulders", i.e. the upper surface of the semi-cylindrical body, are slightly more angular. Both pieces appear to have simple curvilinear marks painted on them (Fig. 56, right

Fig. 58. Reverse of a stone grave stela and its base from Tarut.

side; Fig. 58, on the head, lower body, and base). Whether these are original or applied in the recent past we do not know.

Stelae of this sort are also known from Bahrain. According to the late Thomas Barger, the Danish expedition excavated "three stone 'idols'...spaced evenly around a tumulus in Bahrain containing pottery of the Thaj/Jawan type" (letter of T.G. Bibby to Mr. T. Barger, March 3, 1966; Barger, pers. comm.). In 1986, a Franco-Bahraini team under the direction of J.-F. Salles excavated comparable examples in Mound 4 at the necropolis of Karranah, and there are others from Bahrain in the National Museum as well (Salles, pers. comm.).

The coarseware ceramics described by Arnot are a pair of small, straight-rimmed, spouted jars (Fig. 59), and a group of five small, flat-based cups of light buff ware with incurving rim (Fig. 60). Two of these were measured by the author, with the following results: rim diameter 4.7 and 5 cm.; base diameter 3 and 3.3 cm.; height 3.2 and 4.4 cm., respectively. All appear to be local products, but precisely this shape can be found in early Roman Palestine

Fig. 59. Two spouted bowls from Tarut.

Fig. 60. Five flat-based cups from Tarut.

(Andersen 1985:92 and Pl. 10:143, with additional references to examples from Jericho). Undoubtedly, when material from the hundreds of Seleucid and Parthian period graves on Bahrain is published, more comparanda will appear.

This brings us to the glazed pottery found in the Tarut mound. An unknown quantity of glazed pottery was recoverd from the cist graves dug into the Tarut mound, many of which were still intact. We begin with a complete example of a fishplate (Figs. 61-62). The Tarut exemplar has what Hannestad has called "a concave curving on the outer surface" of the rim (cf. Hannestad 1983:28, and Pl. 19:207). The base shows a characteristic, circular depression surrounded, in this case, by a pronounced groove. Most of the glaze was still intact on the Tarut example when it was photographed. While the shape is normally considered a leitfossil of the Hellenistic period, Hannestad has stressed that, at Seleucia, Susa, and on Failaka, it continued to be manufactured into the Parthian period (Hannestad 1983:30). This is certainly the case at ed-Dur, in the U.A.E., where fishplates have been found in first century A.D. contexts

Figs. 61-62. Glazed fishplate from Tarut.

Fig. 63. Carinated bowl from Tarut.

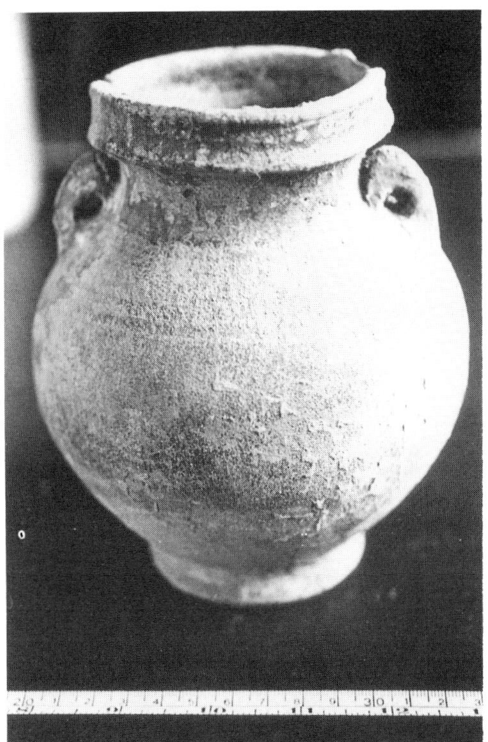

(Boucharlat, Haerinck, Phillips and Potts 1988 and Boucharlat, Haerinck, Lecomte and Potts in press:) in great numbers, or, for example, in level 5d on the Apadana Est at Susa (Boucharlat 1987:198).

A carinated bowl with rounded lip and what looks like a ring base (Fig. 63) belongs to a type well-known from the excavations of the Hellenistic fortress on Failaka. L. Hannestad calls this type a bowl with flaring sides and offset lip (Hannestad 1983:23-25 with further references for comparison and Pl. 8:94-99), and points out that while its origins lie in the Neo-Assyrian period, the form continued in use into the Parthian period.

In addition to these open shapes in glazed ware, a number of closed shapes were recovered from the Tarut mound as well. Four examples (Figs. 64-67) of what Florence Day long ago dubbed the "Mesopotamian amphora" were recovered. Characteristic of the Mesopotamian amphora is either a straight band rim or an everted, stepped rim; a short neck, to which short, thick handles are attached; a squat, oval to round body; and a ring base. Zig-zag decoration in a horizontal panel; vertical striations; or light horizontal indentations may decorate the exterior. This type has recently been studied in detail by L. Hannestad, who points to its rarity on Failaka (Hannestad 1983:Pl. 27, nos. 288-290). In Mesopotamia and Susiana, however, the type is well-known, and

Figs. 64-67. Glazed Mesopotamian amphorae from Tarut.

Fig. 68. Glazed globular bottle from Tarut.

examples can be cited from, *inter alia*, Larsa (Bachelot and Lecomte 1984:Fig. 1:12), Uruk (Strommenger 1967:Taf. 27:12-15, Taf. 40:4; Duda 1979:Taf. 45a, right and 59:104), Assur (Andrae and Lenzen 1933:Taf. 46i), and Susa (Haerinck 1983:Pl. IV:3), to name just a few of the more well-known sites. On Bahrain, the Mesopotamian amphora is among those types which commonly occur in graves of Seleucid-Parthian date (e.g. Bibby 1958:Fig. 5 right, 1969:111, no. 14; During Caspers 1972-74:Fig. 6b, 7c). As Hannestad has stressed, the form was current during both the Seleucid and the Parthian periods (Hannestad 1983:37).

Along with these pieces, a single example of a loop-handled, globular bottle (Fig. 68) is presented here. This form has also been studied exhaustively by L. Hannestad. Pieces comparable to the Tarut bottle are known in the Gulf both on Bahrain (e.g. During Caspers 1972-74:Fig. 7e) and on Failaka (Hannestad 1983:Pl. 29, nos. 301-306), while in Mesopotamia and Susiana the type is well-represented (e.g. Strommenger 1967:Taf. 27:4-7; Duda 1978:Taf. 27e; Valtz 1985:122 and 196, no. 76; Boucharlat 1987:208, Tableau 22).

Dhahran-Dammam

We move now to the area between Dhahran and Dammam where a number of interesting finds have been recorded. The first piece to be presented is a reddish-tan, tripod-based bowl with a ledge rim (Figs. 69-70). The vessel has an interior rim diameter of 22.2 cm.; exterior rim diameter of 25 cm.; and a height of c. 7 cm. The tripod-based bowl is a type well-attested in the region. It is known from Ayn Jawan (Bowen 1950:Fig. 22H); Qalat al-Bahrain (Bibby 1958:Fig. 4 right = 1969:111, no. 13; Boucharlat 1986a:440, Fig. 150:14); and Failaka (Hannestad 1983:Pl. 41, no. 405). All of these vessels were made of a local redware, and we can almost certainly regard the tripod-based bowl as an indigenous, east Arabian type.

The last miscellaneous item from this region is a fragment of architectural decoration (Fig. 71), measuring roughly 1 m. in length, which was recovered from the ruins of a small building. The owner reports, "An isolated mound existed about 50 feet in diameter and about 15 feet in height and located about one mile south west of Khobar in a heavy sand dune area. The mound was located between Thugba and Khobar in the path of a lot of foot traffic....The cornice piece was recovered from the slope of the mound. Rather large slabs of bluish grey fine grained limestone (probably from the rim rock outcrop south west of the Airport) protruded through the sand at the top of the mound". The owner suggests that the decoration on the cornice "was molded in stucco on a slab of farush" (i.e. beachrock).

Figs. 69-70. Tripod-based bowl from the Dhahran-Dammam area.

Fig. 71. Fragment of molded stucco architectural decoration.

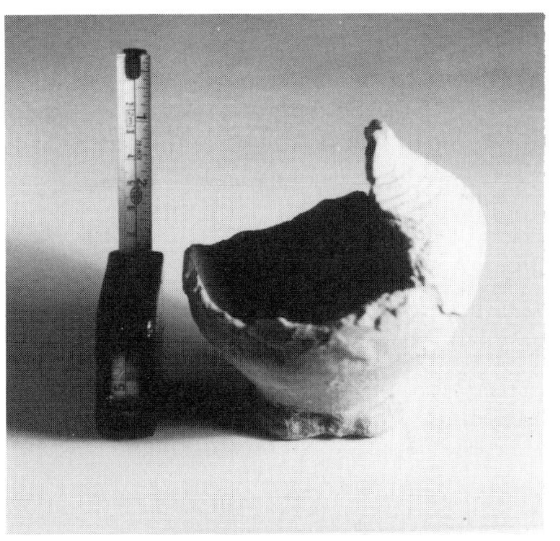

Figs. 72-73. The jar in which the Dhahran jewellery hoard was found.

Two Jewellery Hoards from Dhahran

During the Seleucid period, the inhabitants of northeastern Arabia accumulated vast amounts of wealth. Literary sources leave us in no doubt about the fact that the focus of economic activity in the region was the emporium of Gerrha, and Strabo reckoned the Gerrhaeans, along with the Sabaeans, to be the richest of all the Arabs (*Geog.* 16,4,19). Nowhere is the extent of that wealth better illustrated than in Polybius' account (*Hist.* XIII,9,4-5) of the "gift of five hundred talents of silver, a thousand talents of frankincense, and two hundred talents of the so-called 'stacte'" which the Gerrhaeans bestowed upon Antiochus III in return for their "perpetual peace and freedom". The visible signs of this enormous wealth have, however, been slow to appear, even though a number of silver coin issues attributed to northeastern Arabia surely reflect the existence of a not insignificant amount of disposable wealth. Now, however, we are able to make known to scholars and interested laymen the discovery of two hoards of jewellery from Dhahran which significantly transform our image of Seleucid society in al-Hasa.

In 1969 a small jar (Figs. 72-73) was found inverted on the surface of a mound located southwest of a small, pentagonal fort on the large site south of the Dhahran Airport (cf. Potts et al. 1978:15-18 and Pl. 2 for a plan of the site; Pl. 3A for a plan of the pentagonal fort). The find was made close to the remains of a building which had been partially excavated by local amateurs (a portion of the plaster facade of the building, revealing a niche and a brown and blue/grey painted floral motif (Fig. 74), had been cleared). The jar was exposed after a rainstorm, and contained a sizable hoard of jewellery (Fig. 75). The author has not had the opportunity to examine this material first

Fig. 74. Painted ornamentation on the plastered facade of a building on the Dhahran Airport site.

hand, and has worked solely from photographs and general descriptions provided by a friend of the owner's. There is, however, not the slightest doubt concerning either the authenticity of the find or its locus of discovery.

Let us begin with beads. These were all found loose in the soil around the jar, and originally included several which may have been pearls. These, however, disintegrated rapidly when exposed to the atmosphere. Three of the beads seem to be made of shell or bone (Fig. 75, bottom row left). As many as twenty of the stone beads appear to be made of garnet or amethyst. The larger ones (Fig. 75, center; bottom row of stone beads) look to be of the common,

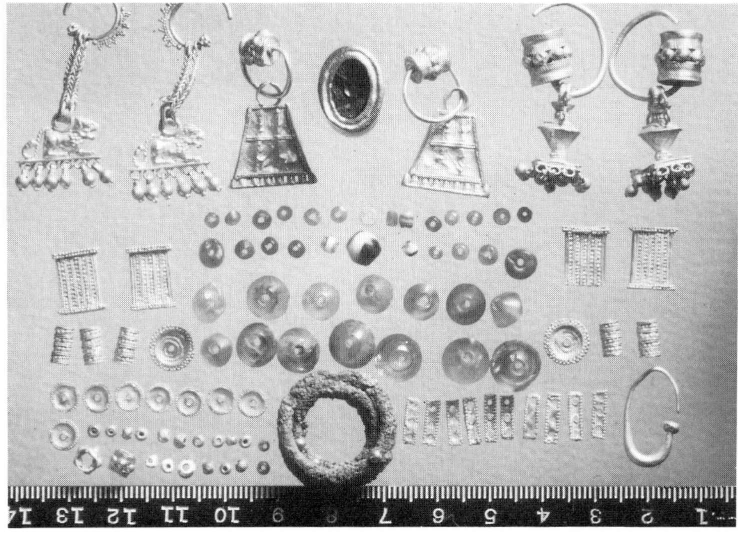

Fig. 75. The Dhahran hoard.

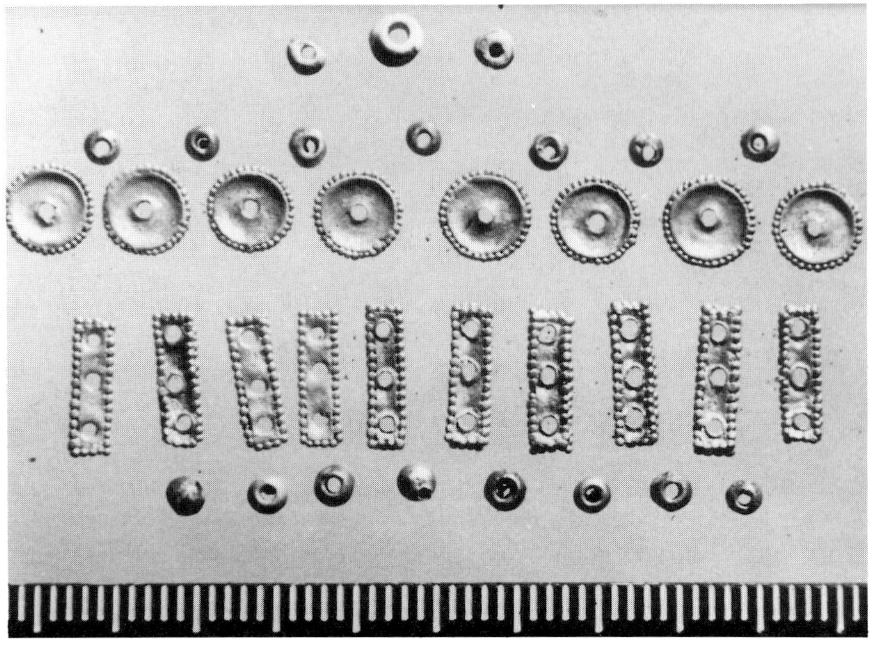

Fig. 76. A selection of gold beads from the Dhahran hoard.

Fig. 77. Saucer-shaped gold bead from Dhahran with granulated border.

Fig. 78. A selection of gold beads from the Dhahran hoard.

Fig. 79. Fancy cylinder gold bead from the Dhahran hoard.

Fig. 80. Gold plaque from the Dhahran hoard. Fig. 81. Gold plaque from the Dhahran hoard.

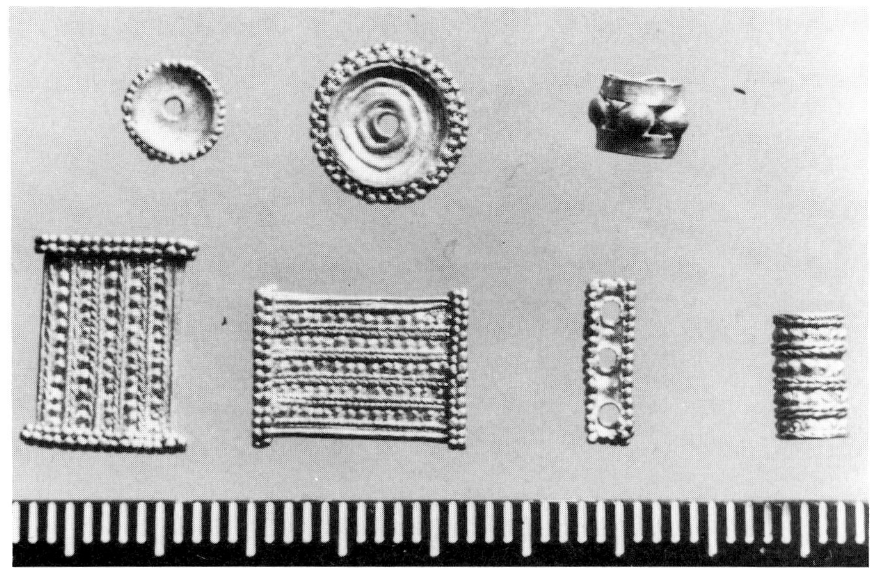

biconical type. Three or four of the beads (Fig. 75, center; first and second row of stone beads) appear to be made of banded agate, and are barrel-shaped. The rest, judging from a color photograph, are most probably made of carnelian or chalcedony. These appear to be barrels, spheres, and rings (cf. for the vocabulary of bead description, Beck 1927, and Brunton 1928:16-20).

We turn now to the simpler gold beads. These include fifteen which are simple, rather thick rings (Fig. 76, second and fifth rows). Next we have eight saucer-shaped disks with granulation around the edge (Fig. 76, third row; 77, upper left). The interior plane of this type is flat and smooth. A more complex variant of this same sort has a double row of border granulation, and grooving on the interior (Fig. 78, 77 middle of the top row). Two beads are made up of thin, hollow cylinders with five round knobs ringing the center (Fig. 75, bottom left; 77, upper right).

Next we come to the more complex gold beads and ornaments. This includes five specimens of what Brunton would probably have classified as "fancy cylinders" (Fig. 79; 77, lower right; 75, center, far left and right). These beads consist of a cylinder with four double rows and one single row of twisted rope decoration, between which are four horizontal rows of raised dots. Judging by the photographs, these are approximately 7 mm. long and

just over 3 m. in diameter. Among the ornamental pieces which cannot be classified as beads we have two sorts of small gold plaques. The first type (Fig. 80; 77, bottom row, second from right; 75, bottom row, right) is represented by ten examples. These are narrow, flat rectangles with a border of granulation. They are perforated by three holes and were probably meant to be sewn onto a garment. Next we find four larger rectangular plaques (Fig. 81; 77, bottom row left; 75, center, right and left) which are made up of two vertical rows of granulation on each short side; six rows of twisted rope decoration running horizontally (i.e. perpendicular to the vertical rows of granulation); and five rows of raised dots. The photographs show no visible means by which these could have been attached to anything.

We turn now to the earrings. The hoard contains three pairs of matched earrings, as well as part a single earring (Fig. 75, bottom righthand corner). The finial of this curving loop of gold is broad, flat, and undecorated. It was obviously meant to prevent a gold bead, through which the upper part of the loop would have been passed, from slipping off. Thus, we see only the plain body of an earring here, minus its decorative element (cf. below, for an earring from the second find in which a granulated bead was found mounted on a similar loop). It is possible that the two hollow cylindrical beads with a central band of raised dots (Fig. 75, bottom left; 78, upper right), mentioned above, originally hung from loops of this sort (as shown in Fig. 82, but not found in this way).

Three elegant pairs of earrings constitute the pride of this hoard. Each is made up of at least three main components. The first pair (Figs. 83-84) consists of a simple gold loop, the finial of which, apparently soldered on, is a large, cylindrical bead with lightly engraved diagonal strokes along four raised ridges, and a row of raised dots ringing its center. This loop passes through a ring on top of a complex pendant with a short neck, decorated with granulation and flanked by two pairs of flat gold rings, one above the other, the whole of which rests on a large biconical section, bordered at the base by another ring of granulation. This portion of the earring resembles generally an amphora or carinated, ceramic vase (see below). At the base of this element is a flat square with rings soldered onto its underside, and from these hang approximately ten pomegranate-shaped beads, each with a thin wire loop on it for attachment.

The second pair of earrings (Fig. 85-86) is constructed like the first of an identical gold loop with a cylindrical bead finial. From this hangs a trapezoidal plaque with ring attachment. The sides of each trapezoid are decorated with fine chasing; the base has a twisted rope border; and the bottom of the trapezoid has of a row of seven vertical cylinders soldered into it. The surface of each side of the plaque is divided into two registers by a pair of braided bands. In each space we see lightly embossed nearly identical scenes. The

Fig. 82. Gold earring with attached beads from the Dhahran hoard.

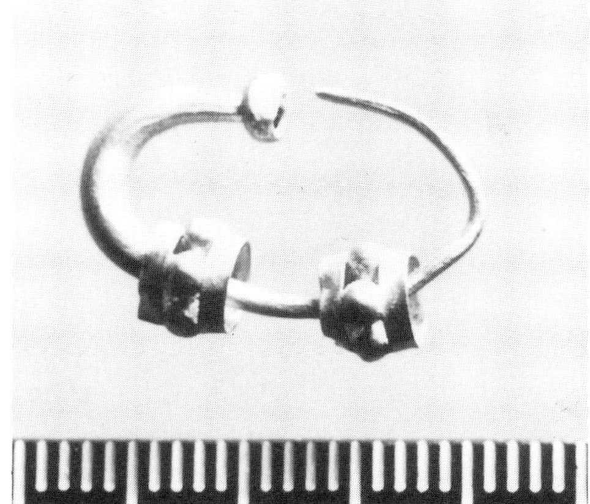

Figs. 83-84. Pair of gold earrings with vase-shaped element from the Dhahran hoard.

Figs. 85-86. Pair of gold earrings with pendant plaques from the Dhahran hoard.

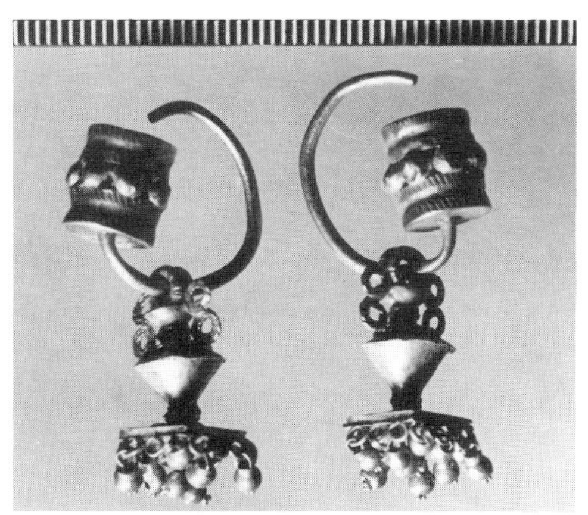

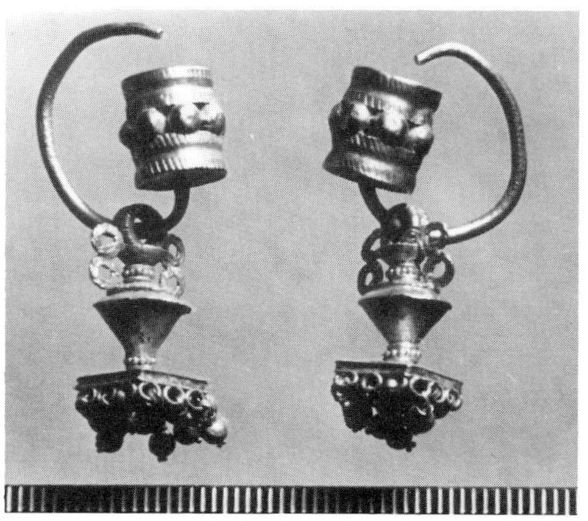

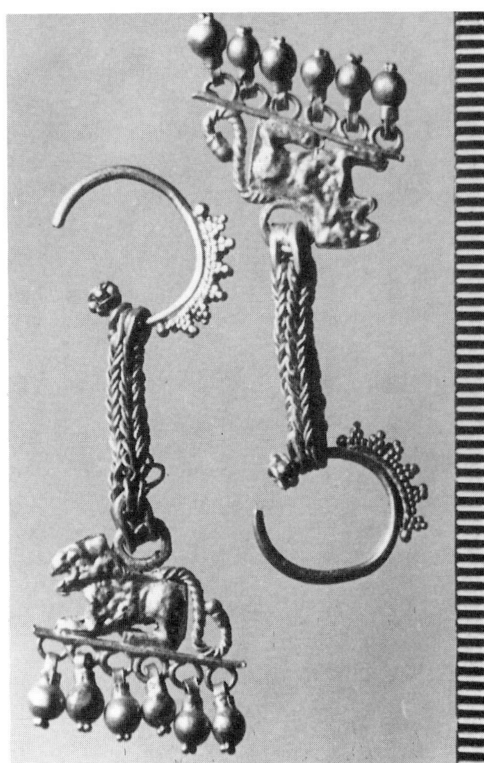

Fig. 87. Gold earrings with crouching lions and pomegranate beads from the Dhahran hoard.

Fig. 88. Close-up of the lions and pomegranates.

Fig. 89 (opposite, left). Side view of a gold ring with inlaid garnet from the Dhahran hoard.

Fig. 90 (opposite, right). Close-up of the bezel and carved garnet of the ring in the Dhahran hoard.

upper register contains two human figures, one of which (e.g. Fig. 85, upper left) appears to be slightly stooped with his arms held up in front of him, facing a second standing figure (difficult to see). The lower register shows, facing in opposite decoration, a crouching winged animal, perhaps a sphinx. These scenes are apparently repeated on both sides of each plaque, although it is difficult to be certain from the available photographs.

But by far the most magnificent pieces in the hoard are a pair of lion earrings (Figs. 87-88). Each consists of a loop of gold with granulation resembling a stepped battlement along half of the outer edge, and a short cylinder with raised dot decoration as a finial. From this is suspended a braided double gold chain which is attached to a ring on the back of a crouching lion. The lion's tail is in each case braided. The rendering of his body shows careful attention to the musculature of the hindquarters; raised dots on the shoulders; clearly marked cheeks, eyes, and triangular ears; an open jaw; and a protruding tongue running down along the base of the lion's mouth. The lions are supported on a narrow, flat strip of gold, to the bottom of which were soldered six rings. Each of these supports a pomegranate-shaped bead with flat loop attachment.

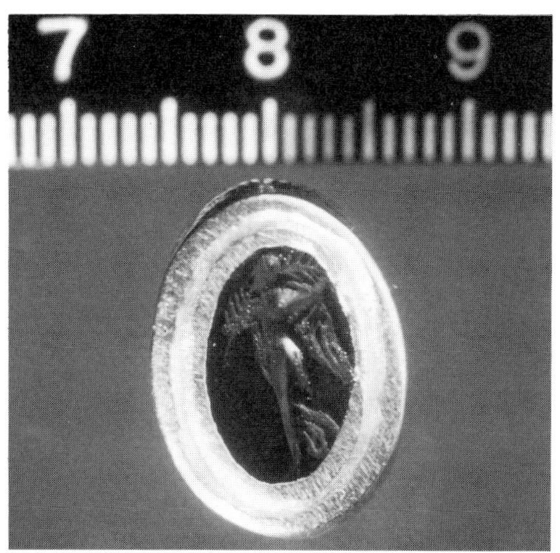

The remainder of the hoard consists of a corroded ring of silver to which at least three small gold beads were still attached (Fig. 75, bottom center), and a gold ring with an engraved garnet still in situ (Fig. 75, top center; 89-90). The ring has an oval bezel, perpendicular shoulders, and a groove around its upper surface. The gem shows a helmeted, winged Nike/Victory carrying a palm frond over her right shoulder.

The contents of the Dhahran hoard appear to be relatively homogeneous, and do not suggest a mélange of material collected over time. If we assume, therefore, that most of the contents are roughly contemporary, we can turn perhaps most securely to the ring and engraved gem for an approximate date. The same bezel and shape is found on a gold ring in the Ashmolean Museum dated to the second half of the third or first half of the second century B.C. (Boardman and Vollenweider 1978:Pl. LVI-LVII:342). A similar gem showing Nike/Victory, on a ring in the British Museum, is dated generally to the Hellenistic period (Marshall 1907:Pl. XII:381 and Walters 1926:Pl. XVII:1171). Gold earrings of considerable complexity are also well-known from this time, and a third century B.C. *kurgan* at Ryzanowka yielded a pair with griffins shown crouching in much the same attitude as the Dhahran lions (Hadaczek 1903:41 and Fig. 76). Braided gold chains, similar to those shown here, are also known in Hellenistic jewellery (e.g. Hoffmann and Davidson 1965:Figs. 5, 19a, 20, 42, 48, and 51; Higgins 1980:Pl. 48D). The first set of earrings (Figs. 83-84) with the amphora-shaped central element, belong to a class of Late Hellenistic and Roman earrings on which "vase-shaped drops, either of amphora or less commonly of oinochoe form" are found (Turner 1973:130, with further refs.). In the Greco-Roman world, these vessel-shaped drops are usually rounded in profile (cf. the long discussion in Kraay and Moorey 1969:202-203, with extensive bibliography), while an example in the Muncherjee

Collection (Aden Museum) shows an angular, carinated shape with a double set of handles attached to the neck and a cylinder bead finial, much like the one from Dhahran (Turner 1973:Pl. XLIX:J). A hoard of jewellery found at Pasargadae included earrings, dated by the excavator to the fourth century, with pendant pomegranate-shaped beads (Stronach 1978:176, Fig. 85:1, Pl. 148a) much like those seen here in the Dhahran hoard (Figs. 83-84, 87-88). Thus, it seems not unlikely that the contents of the Dhahran hoard should be dated at the earliest to the late fourth, but more probably to the third or early second century B.C. Seen historically, it is likely that the hoard would date to sometime on either side of 200 B.C., given the enormous wealth which, according to ancient sources (see above), the Gerrhaeans amassed at that time.

Although it is of no as yet ascertainable chronological value, a number of parallels can be drawn between the contents of the Dhahran hoard and finds of gold jewellery in the Muncherjee Collection, Aden Museum. This particularly concerns the less immediately diagnostic gold beads. Thus, both the simple and more elaborate varieties of saucer-shaped beads (Figs. 76-77) are found in the South Arabian group (cf. Turner 1973:Pl. LIV:40, 43).

Approximately one kilometer away from the pentagonal fort, in the direction of al-Khobar, another find was made. "Again, the ground was damp from recent rains and surface material was sparse. I was attracted to a small patch of very brightly colored sand - red, yellow, blue, green - so I scratched the surface - the colors continued - I continued finding nothing but more color but about 16-18" the find came to light - nothing else, and the colors ended". This find included three corroded silver bracelets (Figs. 91-93). One of these (Fig. 93) is nearly a double coil, the finials of which have been bent back to form an open loop at each end (in other cases, finials such as these which have been bent back are often decorated as animals' heads, e.g. Maxwell-Hyslop 1971:Pl. 161). Another has a single bent loop at one end (Fig. 92). The third (Fig. 93) belongs to a well-known type of bracelet in which the terminals have a wider diameter (and are often decorated, e.g. Maxwell-Hyslop 1971:Pl. 162) than the rest of the bracelet. No decoration is visible in this case, but an example of a lead bracelet with incised decoration at each end was found in one of the Dhahran tombs in 1977 (Potts et al. 1978:Pl. 10:52). All three of these bracelets are described as being "child size".

Along with the silver objects, the second find consisted of three gold earrings and a bracelet. The earrings are all types represented in the main hoard. These include a solitary loop with bulbous finial (Fig. 94, cf. Fig. 75, lower righthand corner); a loop with flattened finial, threaded through a cylindrical bead with granulated borders and raised dots around the middle (Fig. 95, cf. Fig. 82); and a single example of a lion earring (Fig. 96, cf. Figs. 87-88). The lion in the second find differs from those in the main hoard in several re-

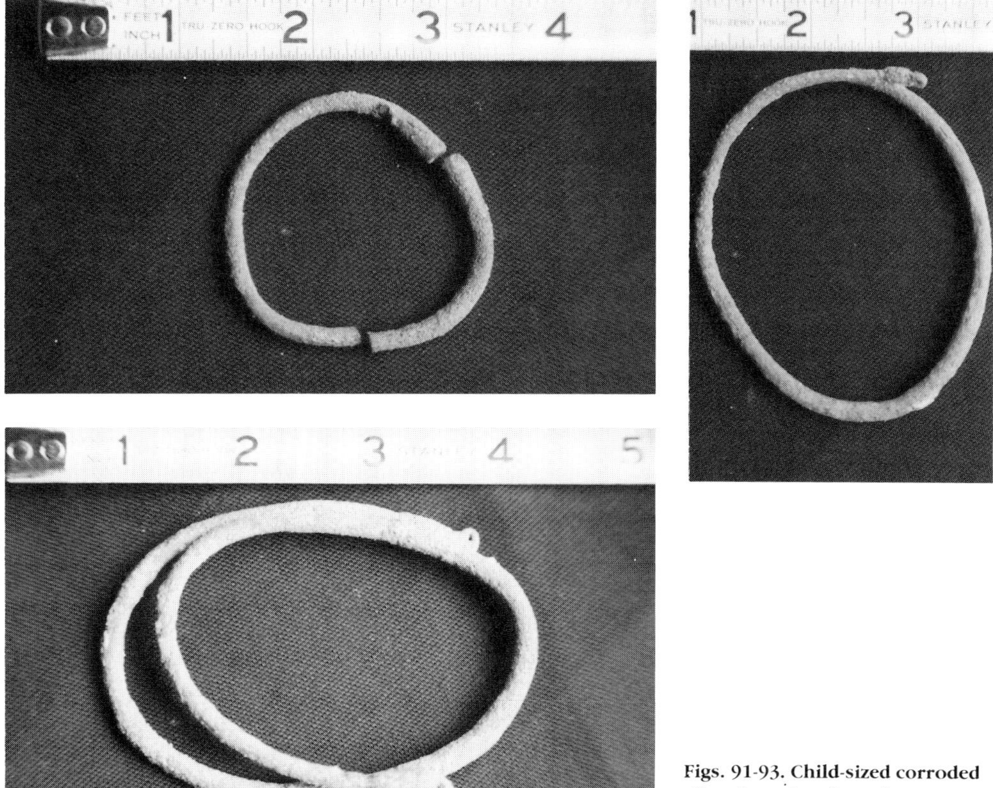

Figs. 91-93. Child-sized corroded silver bracelets from the second Dhahran jewellery find.

spects. To begin with, the braiding of the tail is said to be less "elegantly twisted". Secondly, its tail protrudes from its mouth much more. In all other ways, however, these are clearly identical and undoubtedly come from the same hand or workshop.

The final item in the second find is a magnificent gold bracelet with ibex-headed finials (Fig. 97). The body of the bracelet is a hollow strip of sheet gold, possibly filled with some foreign matter, which was folded and soldered along a clearly visible seam. The terminals are probably solid gold, and are described as being heavier than the bracelet. The bracelet itself seems to fit into the finials, and has a smaller diameter than they do. A simple band of granulated decoration trims the bottom of the ibex necks. The heads are slender and finely rendered, the eyes large and ovoid, the ears swept back like a bird's wing. The horns are unusually long , running straight back from the head and joining the main body of the bracelet. The mouth is indicated by a lightly engraved line. There is no indication of a beard or hair of any kind on the ibex's chin and throat.

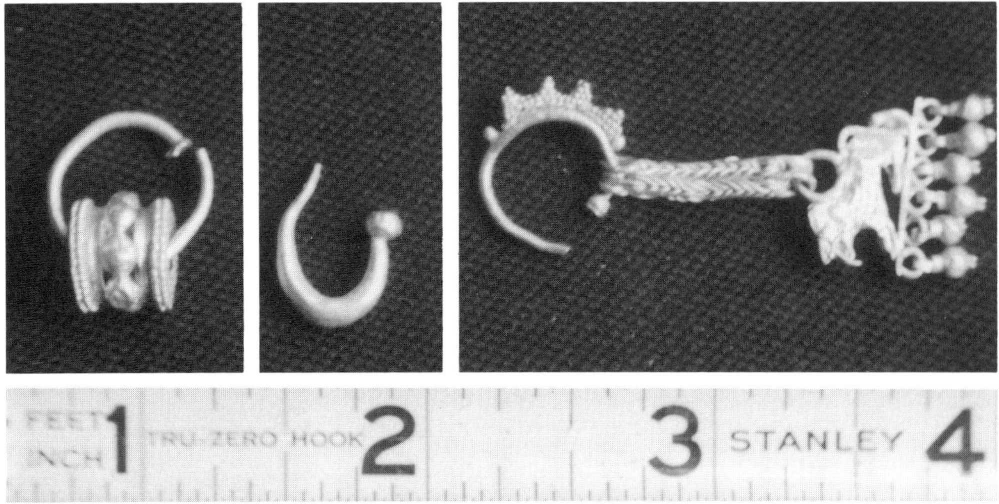

Figs. 94. Gold earring with attached bead from the second Dhahran find.

Fig. 95. Gold loop from the second Dhahran find.

Fig. 96. Gold earring with crouching lion and pomegranate beads from the second Dhahran find.

In publishing an important pair of gold, ibex-headed bracelets from a hoard discovered at Pasargadae, D. Stronach made an extensive study of this genre in the late Achaemenid period (Stronach 1978:173-175, and Fig. 85:4, Pl. 146d and 147). Many of the characteristics of these bracelets, such as the treatment of the beard; the set of the eyes and eyebrows; or the upright posture of the

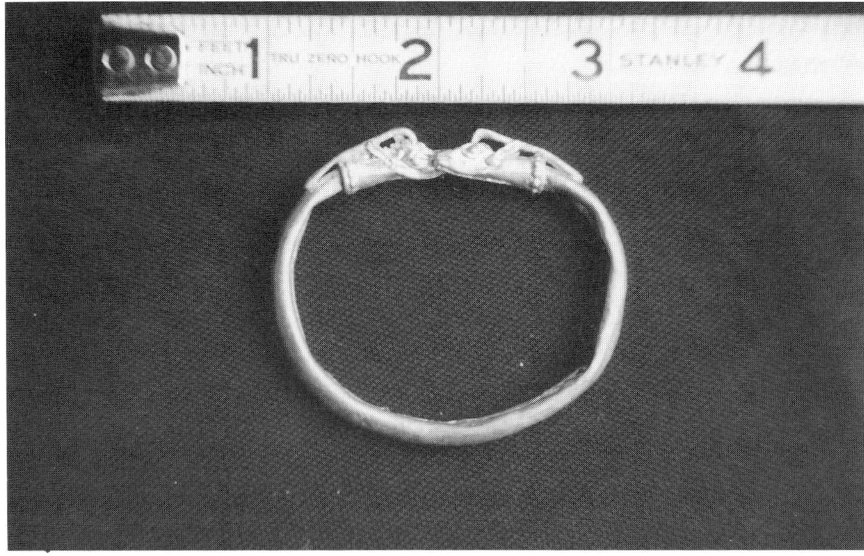

Fig. 97. Gold bracelet with ibex-headed finials from the second Dhahran find.

ears, are lacking on the Dhahran example. Stronach, however, points to the tendency to elongate the heads in later examples, and in this respect the Dhahran piece would seem to be a late product. This fact, along with the replacement of the traditional Achaemenid twisted wire bracelet by a smooth, solid one, suggests a post-Achaemenid date, and indeed bracelets with antelope or ibex-headed finials are known in the Hellenistic period (e.g. Hoffmann and Davidson 1965:161-162). For these reasons, a Hellenistic date seems most appropriate for the Dhahran bracelet, and consequently for the second find in general.

A Tomb South of Dhahran Airport

P.B. Cornwall was the first to proclaim the significance of the thousands of burial mounds which once ringed the Dammam dome (e.g. Cornwall 1943:231; 1946:35-37 and especially Pl. 2 with an aerial view of tumuli north of 'Ain as Saih; and 1948:513). Despite the fact that their numbers have been severely diminished by the construction of the Dhahran Airport, hundreds of these mounds still exist and the impression they make on a visitor (Figs. 98-99) is identical to that of the more well-known and indeed more numerous mounds on Bahrain. A number of these mounds have been excavated scientifically in recent years (Potts et al. 1978:18, Pl. 4 for the plan and sections, Pl. 10 for the contents of one; Zarins et al. 1984), and some have been opened by amateurs. Here, we are able to report on one such mound, excavated in March, 1964.

Figs. 98-99. General views of the Dhahran tumuli.

Figs. 100-101. Excavation of a mound in the Dhahran field, March, 1964.
Fig. 102. View into one of the chambers of the Dhahran grave. Fig. 103. Four crania in the Dhahran grave.

The excavation of the mound was carried out by a small team, who cut a slit through the earthen mantle of the mound (Figs. 100-101) in an effort to gain entry into the stone-built tomb chamber. This was achieved, and the excavators came into what has been described as "a single room with rock and mud walls with a domed roof" (Fig. 102). In light of what we know of the Dhahran mounds from other excavations, it seems certain that the roof was not domed, but rather that the excavators entered one portion of what was probably a T-shaped burial chamber (cf. Potts et al. 1978:Pl. 4). The grave contained the remains of at least four individuals, the crania of which were more or less intact (Fig. 103). Personal ornaments included hundreds of semi-precious stone (agate, carnelian) and paste (frit, faience) beads of various sorts (Fig. 104), sometimes still lying in situ as necklaces (Fig. 105). A variety of bronze ornaments, including rings and bracelets; various utensils (Fig. 106); razors and points (Fig. 107); and a large pin with an etched herringbone design (Fig. 108), were also recovered. A small selection of iron objects,

Fig. 104. Selection of beads from the Dhahran grave.

Fig. 105. A necklace shown in situ in the Dhahran grave (scale is an American quarter, c. 2.4 cm. in diameter).

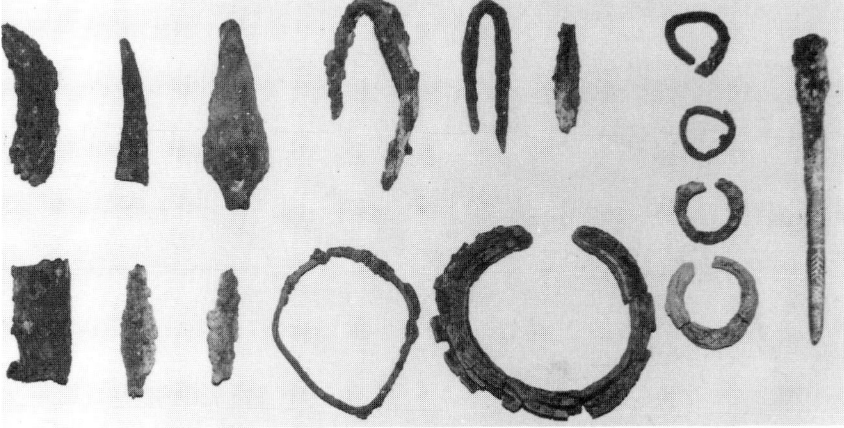

Fig. 106. Selection of bronze and iron (top and bottom rows, far left) objects from the Dhahran grave.

Fig. 107. Bronze points and razors from the Dhahran grave.

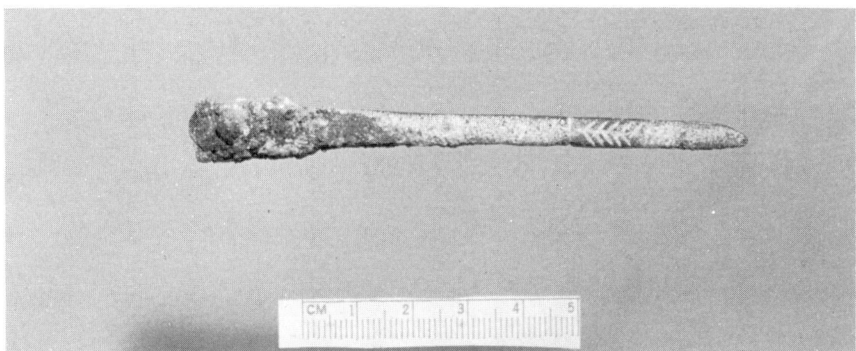

Fig. 108. Incised bronze pin from the Dhahran grave.

Fig. 109. Iron objects from the Dhahran grave.

including a bent nail and a heavy bolt (Fig. 109) may have been fittings for objects, such as boxes or wooden shields, which may have originally been placed in the grave.

The ceramic and stone finds were not numerous but are of some interest. A large, glazed amphora with twisted handles (Figs. 110-111) is probably Parthian. It has an everted rim with an indented ridge below it; horizontal striations along the middle of the neck; and pronounced ridges around the middle of a stout, ovoid body. The vessel has a ring-base. Twisted handles are also found, for instance, on amphorae from Parthian Assur, where however the body decoration is more ornate (e.g. Andrae and Lenzen 1933:Taf. 46h, k; cf. Debevoise 1935:Pl. I:2-4). On the other hand, the general appearance of this vessel is not so unlike a glazed amphora, dated to the fifth century, from Sasanian Choche (Ricciardi 1985:133 and 204, no. 164). In any case, the vessel presented here finds an exact parallel in two fragmentary amphorae found in another Dhahran grave excavated in 1977 (Potts et al. 1978:Pl. 10:43-44). This grave, moreover, contained an alabaster unguent jar which strongly recalls one found in the grave under discussion (see below).

It is instructive to compare the obviously imported, glazed amphora with the common ware of the region, as seen in Figs. 112-114. These are of a crudeness which almost defies belief. The fabric is in all cases soft, poorly fired, and full of chaff. One of these vessels (Fig. 112) shows plastic ridges on

Fig. 110. A glazed amphora in the Dhahran grave during excavation.

Fig. 111. The Dhahran grave amphora.

Figs. 112-114. Coarseware vessels from the Dhahran grave.

its shoulder and body, while another (Fig. 113) has the faintest indication of a lip for pouring.

We come finally to a small alabaster unguent jar (Figs. 115-116), equipped with four vertical nose lugs, and a double row of crudely incised diagonal lines around the rim. The accompanying lid has a sloping, perforated handle. This sort of jar is now well-known in Arabia. Comparable examples have been found at Thaj (Bibby 1966:150, where the handle of the lid is in the form of a crouching lion); Qaryat al-Fau (Al-Ansary 1982:74-75, Pls. 2, 4); Mleiha (Boucharlat 1986b:Fig. 33:1-4); Timna (Cleveland 1965:Pl. 89:TC 1951, with shorter lugs); and in the Dhahran tomb excavated in 1977 (Potts et al. 1978:Pl. 10:50, with an incised human face).

Figs. 115-116. Alabaster unguent jar and lid from the Dhahran grave.

Jabal Kenzan

We move further south now to Jabal Kenzan, a site already introduced in this study (cf. Chapter II). A trilobate arrowhead picked up here (Fig. 117) can be compared generally with finds from Persepolis, Pasargadae (Stronach 1978:Fig. 94), Susa (Boucharlat 1987:294, with additional references, and Fig. 78:1, 3, late Seleucid), or Janussan (Lombard and Salles 1984:Fig. 8:1-2). It is difficult, however, to suggest a date for the Jabal Kenzan piece, as this type of arrowhead, after making its appearance in the late Achaemenid period, continued in use into the Sasanian era (cf. Cleuziou 1977:189-196).

A more unusual find from Jebel Kenzan is a hollow, cast bronze handle in the form of a horse protome (Figs. 118-119). Only the front legs of the leaping horse are damaged. Otherwise, the body of the object terminates at the withers, and was intended to be mounted on something. It is difficult to know just what the function of this item was. Identical horse protomes have now been found in a first century A.D. grave at ed-Dur (C.S. Phillips, pers. comm., season of 1988); in grave 2020 at Site 20 in Samad ash-Shan (Yule and Weisgerber 1988:Fig. 8:6); and Mleiha (Boucharlat 1986b:Fig. 34:2). A bronze handle terminating in a lion protome from Kermanshah (cf. Porada 1964:no. 472), which has been dated to the first-third centuries A.D., may offer a clue. On the other hand, a hollow bronze lion protome from Iron Age Hasanlu

Fig. 117. Trilobate bronze arrowhead from Jabal Kenzan. Figs. 118-119. Cast bronze horse protome from Jabal Kenzan.

The Sasanian Period

CHAPTER V

The history of al-Hasa during the Sasanian period is relatively well-known for certain eras, such as the reigns of Ardashir, Shapur II, or Khusraw II, thanks to later Arab and Persian sources, especially Tabari. A patchwork political history of the region's relations with the Laẖmid and Kinda dynasties can also be reconstructed, and the often eventful history of the Nestorian church of Beṯ Qatraye, as the region was known in ecclesiastical sources, has been reviewed on more than one occasion (see the extensive discussion with bibliography in Potts, in press a, vol. II). The archaeological investigation of this important epoch has, however, lagged far behind the study of its historical sources, and very few remains, apart from a hoard of Sasanian dirhams from Tarut (Al-Mughannum 1983) and a group of Sasanian coins in an early Islamic hoard from al-Khobar (Morris 1975), have come to light during the past forty years.

Although the selection of Sasanian objects published here is small, it nevertheless represents a not insignificant addition to what is presently known of the Sasanian presence, as attested archaeologically, in the area. We begin with a Sasanian stamp seal (Fig. 122) of garnet picked up on the surface, near the edge of an old camp fire, roughly 4.5 kms. northwest of Dammam. The seal depicts a crouching lion, facing the viewer, with both mane and paws rendered in a simple, sketchy manner. Lions in a similar

Fig. 122. Sasanian stamp seal of garnet found northwest of Dammam.

Fig. 123. Sasanian (?) coarseware jar with incised decoration from the Dhahran Airport site.

attitude were a favorite subject of Sasanian seal cutters, and many comparanda are known (e.g. Delaporte 1920:Pl. 55:71-72, D. 224-225; Delaporte 1923:Pl. 110:27, 33-34, 36-37, A. 1378, 1383-1389; Von der Osten 1957:No. 227; Frye 1973:D. 37, 69, 154, 174, 181, 355, 442; or Gignoux 1977:Pl. XII:4.56 and Pl. XXIX:9.64).

From the surface of the Dhahran Airport site comes a tall pink jar (Fig. 123) with a buff surface and incised decoration around the neck and shoulder. This consists of horizontal and wavy incised lines around the middle of the body, and horizontal lines around the neck. The jar stands 33.5 cm. tall and has a ring base with a diameter of 6.7 cm.; an interior rim diamter of 7.7 cm.; and an exterior rim diameter of 9.4 cm. It is difficult to be certain whether or not this vessel is pre-Islamic, but the incised decoration on an unglazed body recalls, for example, decorated coarseware jars from a number of Sasanian sites (e.g. de Cardi 1972:Fig. 2:23, 29 34; Whitcomb 1984:Fig. 2-3; Whitcomb 1987:Fig. D:s, hh).

Fig. 124. Face of a Sasanian stamp seal from Darin.

Fig. 125. Impression of the seal shown in Fig. 124.

Figs. 126-127. Obverse and face of a Sasanian stamp seal from Darin.

Fig. 128. Impression of the seal shown in Figs. 126-127.

Fig. 129. Sasanian stucco fragment from Darin.

Darin, on Tarut, is the source of the objects which follow.That this town existed in the Sasanian era is proven beyond doubt by references to it as a Nestorian bishopric as early as 410, when the Nestorian catholicos Mar Isaac appointed one Paul bishop of fthe "islands of *Ardai* and *Todourou* ", i.e. Darin and Tarut (Braun 1900:33; Chabot 1902:273). The very name Darin, moreover, derives from Aramaic *dayr*, meaning "cloister, monastery". Later, we learn that Khusraw II had an interpreter who hailed from Darin (Nöldeke 1893:14), while "travelling merchants from Darin" are mentioned in a verse written by the pre-Islamic Arab poet al-A'sha (Thilo 1958:39).

Around 1965 excavation for a cellar in Darin brought to light two Sasanian stamp seals and a pair of stucco fragments. Once again, the seals show well-known subjects in Sasanian glyptic. The first example (Figs. 124-125) is made of an opaque, grey-green quartz. The form is that of a perforated, rounded hemisphere, a widely represented form in the Sasanian world (Göbl 1973:Taf. 40; cf. generally Debevoise 1934). The seal shows a crouching hare, an animal not uncommon on Sasanian seals (cf. a seal from Tello in the Louvre, Delaporte 1920:Pl. 6:9a-bf, T. 251; Delaporte 1923:Pl. 109:13, A. 1302, for a running hare; Göbl 1973:Taf. 13:38a). The second Darin seal (Figs. 126-128) has the form of a flat disk. It is made of a translucent orange quartz, and shows a standing quadruped with one front leg raised. The rather heavy body and

Fig. 130. Sasanian stucco fragment from Darin.

short legs recall a sheep, but the sketchy mane and raised foreleg suggest a horse (cf. Delaporte 1920:Pl. 55:66-68, D. 219-221 with a similar circle of strokes/dots around a lion).

The same cellar excavation also yielded two fragments of Sasanian stucco. One of these (Fig. 129) shows a couchant ram with well-defined horns, chest fleece, and legs, and vegetation intruding on the right. The whole piece measures 21.5 cm. wide along its top edge, and 19 cm. along the bottom. It is 1.5 cm. thick. "Couchant ruminants" are not infrequent in Sasanian stucco decoration, for example in the Sasanian palace at Kish or the subsidiary palace at Chal Tarkhan, and several examples can be compared with the Darin piece (cf. Kröger 1978:105; Thompson 1976:37 and Pl. X, Fig. 3 (C.212) and Pl. XXII.3). The second fragment (Fig. 132) shows a bird; a large fleur-de-lis; and a lenticular leaf, the whole measuring roughly 17.5 x 17 cm. In both the Sasanian palace at Kish and at Ctesiphon, vegetation was depicted which recalls the fleur-de-lis here (e.g. Kröger 1978:103, Fig. G and 105, no. 37).

Conclusion

The value of the present communication lies, I hope, in the demonstration that unstratified material from generally known provenance is not without value, particularly in an area as poorly investigated as al-Hasa. Political conditions have always determined the freedom of movement and excavation which archaeologists could enjoy in the region, and they continue to do so today. Sadly, this has always been very limited. This being the case, we must indeed be grateful to those ARAMCO members who, over the years, acquired important antiquities from a region in which systematic archaeological investigations have been all too few, and in which the devastation of modernization has been widespread. The testimony of the material presented here, although late in coming to the attention of scholars, is no less important for the reconstruction of the culture history of the region than those rare surveys and excavations conducted by professional archaeologists have been. From the time of Captain Shakespear's visit to Thaj in 1911, to the inception of the Comprehensive Survey of the Kingdom of Saudi Arabia and the excavations which followed it in the 1970's and early 1980's, appallingly little official archaeological work has been carried out in the region. This should encourage us to exploit every shred of evidence, whatever its origin, which throws light on the antiquity of al-Hasa.

Abbreviations

AAW	F. Altheim and R. Stiehl, *Die Araber in der Alten Welt*, de Gruyter, Berlin, 1964-1969.
AJA	*American Journal of Archaeology*
AOMIM	R. Boucharlat and J.-F. Salles, eds., *Arabie Orientale, Mésopotamie et Iran Méridional de l'Age du Fer au début de la période Islamique*, Éditions Recherches sur les Civilisations, Paris, 1984.
AUAE	*Archaeology in the United Arab Emirates*
BaF	*Baghdader Forschungen*
BaM	*Baghdader Mitteilungen*
BASOR	*Bulletin of the American Schools of Oriental Research*
BBVO	*Berliner Beiträge zum Vorderen Orient*
BTA	Shaikha H.A. Al Khalifa and M. Rice, eds., *Bahrain through the ages: the Archaeology*, Kegan Paul International, London, 1986.
CNIP 7	D.T. Potts, ed., *Araby the Blest*, Carsten Niebuhr Institute Publications 7, Copenhagen, 1988.
DAFI	*Cahiers de la Délégation Archéologique Française en Iran*
EW	*East and West*
IrAnt	*Iranica Antiqua*
JASP	*Jutland Archaeological Society Publications*
JOS	*Journal of Oman Studies*
JRAS	*Journal of the Royal Asiatic Society*
MDAI	*Mémoires de la Délégation Archéologique en Iran*
MDP	*Mémoires de la Délégation en Perse*
OIP	*Oriental Institute Publications*
PSAS	*Proceedings of the Seminar for Arabian Studies*
TMO	*Travaux de la Maison de l'Orient*
UVB	*Vorläufiger Bericht über die von dem Deutschen Archäologischen Institut aus Mitteln der Deutschen Forschungsgemeinschaft unternommenen Ausgrabungen in Uruk-Warka*
WVDOG	*Wissenschaftliche Veröffentlichungen der Deutschen Orient-Gesellschaft*

Bibliography

AL-ANSARY, A.R. 1982. *Qaryat al-Fau, A Portrait of Pre-Islamic Civilisation in Saudi Arabia*, Croom Helm, London.

AL-MUGHANNAM, A. 1983. "Sassanian Coins from the Island of Tarout", unpublished lecture, *Bahrain Through the Ages Conference*, Manama.

AMANDRY, P. 1958. "Orfevérie achéménide", *Antike Kunst* I:9-23.

AMIET, P. 1957. "Les intailles orientales de la collection Henri de Genouillac conservées au Musée départemental des Antiquités de Seine-Maritime a Rouen", *Cahiers de Byrsa* VII:35-73.

AMIET, P. 1986. *L'age des échanges inter-iraniens, 3500-1700 avant J.-C.*, Notes et Documents des Musées de France 11, Paris.

ANDERSEN, F.G. 1985. *Shiloh: The Danish Excavations at Tall Sailun, Palestine in 1926, 1929, 1932 and 1963*, Publications of the National Museum Archaeological-Historical Series Vol. XXIII, Copenhagen.

ANDRAE, W. and H. LENZEN. 1933. *Die Partherstadt Assur, WVDOG* 57, Leipzig.

ANONYMOUS. 1975. *An Introduction to Saudi Arabian Antiquities*, Department of Antiquities and Museums, Ministry of Education, Kingdom of Saudi Arabia.

ANONYMOUS. 1983. "Survey and Excavation in 1983", *Atlal* 7:117-118.

ARNOT, P. 1986a. letter of 9 February to the author.

ARNOT, P. 1986b. letter of 30 March to the author.

BACHELOT, L. and O. LECOMTE. 1984. "Nouvelles données sur l'occupation de la Basse Mésopotamie a la fin du premier millénaire a.C.: La céramique séleuco-parthe de Larsa", *AOMIM*:3-25.

BARATTE, F. and F. ZAYADINE. 1987. "Skulpturen im süd-arabischen Stil", in S. Mittmann et al., eds., *Der Königsweg: 9000 Jahre Kunst und Kultur in Jordanien und Palästina*, von Zabern, Mainz, p. 213-215.

BARGER, T.C. 1965. "Cylinder Seal from Saudi Arabia", *Archaeology* 18:231-232.

BARGER, T.C. 1969. "Greek Inscription Deciphered; Seal Found in Arabia", *Archaeology* 22:139.

BARNETT, R.D. 1969. "New Facts about Musical Instruments from Ur", *Iraq* 31:96-103.

BECK, H.C. 1927. "Classification and Nomenclature of Beads and Pendants", *Archaeologia* LXXVII:1-76.

BIBBY, T.G. 1954. "Fem af Bahrains hundrede tusinde gravhøje (Five among Bahrain's Hundred Thousand Grave-Mounds)", *Kuml 1954*:116-141.

BIBBY, T.G. 1958. "Bahrains oldtidshovedstad gennem 4000 år (The hundred-meter section)", *Kuml 1957*:128-163.

BIBBY, T.G. 1966. "Arabiens arkæologi (Arabian Gulf Archeology)", *Kuml 1965*:133-152.

BIBBY, T.G. 1967. "Arabiens arkæologi (Arabian Gulf Archeology)", *Kuml 1966*:75-95.

BIBBY, T.G. 1969. *Looking for Dilmun*, Knopf, New York.

BIBBY, T.G. 1973. *Preliminary Survey in East Arabia 1968, JASP* XII, Copenhagen.

BISCIONE, R. and M.C. BULGARELLI. 1983. "Painted Geometrical Decoration on the Shahr-i Sokhta Buff Ware: Approach to a Systematic Classification", in M. Tosi, ed., *Prehistoric Sistan* 1, IsMEO, Rome, p. 211-258.

BOARDMAN, J. and M.-L. VOLLENWEIDER. 1978. *Catalogue of the Engraved Gems and Finger Rings, Greek and Etruscan [in the Ashmolean Museum]*, Clarendon Press, Oxford.

BOEHMER, R.M. and H.-W. DÄMMER. 1985. *Tell Imlihiye, Tell Zubeidi, Tell Abbas, BaF* 7, Mainz.

BOUCHARLAT, R. 1986a. "Some notes about Qal'at al-Bahrain during the Hellenistic period", *BTA*:435-444.

BOUCHARLAT, R. 1986b. *Archaeological Surveys and Excavations in the Sharjah Emirate, 1986: A Third Preliminary Report*, Lyons.

BOUCHARLAT, R. 1987."Les niveaux post-achéménides a Suse, secteur nord: Fouilles de l'Apadana-Est et de la Ville Royale-Ouest", *DAFI* 15:145-311.

BOUCHARLAT, R., E. HAERINCK, C.S. PHILLIPS

and D.T. Potts. 1988. "Archaeological Reconnaissance at ed-Dur, Umm al-Qaiwain, U.A.E.", *Akkadica* 58:1-26.

Boucharlat, R., E. Haerinck, O. Lecomte and D.T. Potts. in press. "The European Archaeological Expedition to ed-Dur, Umm al-Qaiwain (U.A.E.): An Interim Report on the 1987 and 1988 Seasons", *Mesopotamia* 24.

Boucharlat, R. and P. Lombard. 1985. "The Oasis of Al Ain in the Iron Age: Excavations at Rumeilah 1981-1983", *AUAE* 4:44-73.

Bowen, R.LeB., Jr. 1950. *The Early Arabian Necropolis of Ain Jawan, BASOR* Suppl. 7-9, New Haven.

Braun, O. 1900. *Das Buch der Synhados oder Synodicon Orientale*, Stuttgart and Vienna.

Brunton, G. 1928. *Qau and Badari II*, British School of Archaeology in Egypt, London.

Buchanan, B. 1966. *Catalogue of Ancient Near-Eastern Seals in the Ashmolean Museum*, Vol. I, Clarendon Press, Oxford.

Burkholder, G. 1971. "Steatite Carvings from Saudi Arabia", *Artibus Asiae* 33:306-322.

Burkholder, G. 1972. "Ubaid Sites and Pottery in Saudi Arabia", *Archaeology* 25:264-269.

Burkholder, G. 1974. "An Early Chalcolithic Site in the Eastern Province of Saudi Arabia, a Survey", *AJA* 78:162.

Burkholder, G. 1984. *An Arabian Collection: Artifacts from the Eastern Province*, GB Publications, Boulder City.

Burkholder, G. and M. Golding. 1971. "Surface Survey of Al Ubaid Sites in the Eastern Province of Saudi Arabia", in H. Field, ed., *Contributions to the Anthropology of Saudi Arabia*, Field Research Projects, Coconut Grove, p. 50-55.

Cardi, B. de. 1970. *Excavations at Bampur, A Third Millennium Settlement in Persian Baluchistan, 1966*, Anthropological Papers of the American Museum of Natural History Vol. 51:3, New York.

Cardi, B. de. 1972. "A Sasanian Outpost in Northern Oman", *Antiquity* 46:305-310.

Cardi, B. de, S. Collier and D.B. Doe. 1976. "Excavations and Survey in Oman, 1974-1975", *JOS* 2:101-187.

Caton Thompson, G. 1944. *The Tombs and Moon Temple of Hureidha (Hadhramaut)*, Reports of the Research Committee of the Society of Antiquaries of London No. XIII, London.

Chabot, J.-B. 1902. "*Synodicon Orientale*, ou Recueil de Synodes Nestoriens", *Notices et Extraits des Manuscrits de la Bibliotheque Nationale* 37:1-685.

Cleuziou, S. 1977. "Les pointes de fleches 'scythiques' au Proche et Moyen-Orient", in J. Deshayes, ed., *Le Plateau Iranien et l'Asie Centrale des Origines a la Conquete Islamique*, Éditions du CNRS, Paris, p. 187-199.

Cleuziou, S. n.d. "Excavations at Hili 8: A Preliminary Report on the 4th to 7th Campaigns", *AUAE*, in press.

Cleuziou, S. and B. Vogt. 1985. "Tomb A at Hili North (United Arab Emirates) and Its Material Connections to Southeast Iran and the Greater Indus Valley", in J. Schotsmans and M. Taddei, eds., *South Asian Archaeology 1983*, Vol. I, Naples, p. 249-277.

Cleveland, R.L. 1965. An Ancient South Arabian Necropolis: Objects from the Second Campaign (1951) in the Timna' Cemetery, Johns Hopkins Press, Baltimore.

Cornwall, P.B. 1943. "The Tumuli of Bahrein", *Asia and the Americas* 43:230-234.

Cornwall, P.B. 1946. "Ancient Arabia: Explorations in Hasa, 1940-41", *Geographical Journal* 107:28-50.

Cornwall, P.B. 1948. "In Search of Arabia's Past", *National Geographic Magazine* 93:493-522.

Dalley, S. 1986. "The god Salmu and the winged disc", *Iraq* 48:85-101.

Debevoise, N.C. 1934. "The Essential Characteristics of Parthian and Sasanian Glyptic Art", *Berytus* 1:12-18.

Debevoise, N.C. 1935. "The Oriental Amphora", *Berytus* 2:1-4.

Delaporte, L. 1920. *Catalogue des Cylindres, Cachets et Pierres Gravées de Style Oriental I. Fouilles et Missions*, Librairie Hachette, Paris.

Delaporte, L. 1923. *Catalogue des Cylindres Cachets et Pierres Gravées de Style Oriental II. Acquisitions*, Librairie Hachette, Paris.

Delougaz, P. 1952. *Pottery from the Diyala Region, OIP* LXIII, Chicago.

Donaldson, P. 1984. "Prehistoric Tombs of Ras al-Khaimah", *OrAnt* 23:191-312.

Duda, D. 1978. "Die Keramik aus dem Gebiet des Gareus-Tempels", *UVB* XXVIII46-56.

Duda, D. 1979. "Die Grabung in U/V

XVIII. 30. Kampagne. Die Keramik", *UVB* XXIX/XXX:50-69.

DURING CASPERS, E.C.L. 1971. "The Bull's Head from Barbar Temple II, Bahrain: A Contact with Early Dynastic Sumer", *EW* 21:217-224.

DURING CASPERS, E.C.L. 1972-74. "The Bahrain Tumuli", *Persica* VI:131-156.

EDENS, C. 1988. "The Rub al-Khali 'Neolithic' Revisited: the View from Nadqan", *CNIP* 7:15-43.

FRANKFORT, H. 1939. *Sculpture of the Third Millennium B.C. from Tell Asmar and Khafajah, OIP* XLIV, Chicago.

FRANKFORT, H. 1943. *More Sculpture from the Diyala Region, OIP* LX, Chicago.

FRIFELT, K. 1969. "Arkæologiske Undersøgelser på Oman Halvøen (Archaeological investigations in the Oman peninsula)", *Kuml 1968*:159-175.

FRIFELT, K. 1971. "Jamdat Nasr fund fra Oman (Jamdat Nasr graves in the Oman)", *Kuml 1970*:355-383.

FRIFELT, K. 1975. "On Prehistoric Settlement and Chronology of the Oman Peninsula", *EW* 25:359-424.

FRIFELT, K. 1979. "The Umm an-Nar and Jemdet Nasr of Oman and their Relations Abroad", in J.E. van Lohuizen-de Leeuw, ed., *South Asian Archaeology 1975*, Brill, Leiden, p. 43-60.

FRYE, R.N. 1973. *Sasanian Remains from Qasr-i Abu Nasr*, Harvard University Press, Cambridge.

GALL, H. VON. 1980. "Relieffragment eines elymäischen Königs aus Masged-e Soleiman", *IrAnt* 15:241-250.

GHIRSHMAN, R. 1976. *Terrasses Sacrées de Bard-e Nechandeh et Masjid-i Solaiman, MDAI* XLV, Paris.

GIGNOUX, P. 1978. *Catalogue des Sceaux, Camées et Bulles Sasanides de la Bibliotheque Nationale et du Musée du Louvre II. Les Sceaux et Bulles Inscrits*, Bibliotheque Nationale, Paris.

GLOB, P.V. 1959. "Arkæologiske Undersøgelser i Fire Arabiske Stater (Archeological Investigations in Four Arab States)", *Kuml 1959*: 233-239.

GLOB, P.V. 1960. "Danske Arkæologer i den Persiske Golf (Danish Archeologists in the Persian Gulf)", *Kuml 1960*: 208-213.

GÖBL, R. 1973. *Der sasanidische Siegelkanon*, Handbuch der mittelasiatischen Numismatik Bd. IV, Braunschweig.

GOLDING, M. 1974. "Evidence for Pre-Seleucid Occupation of East Arabia", *PSAS* 4:19-31.

GOLDING, M. 1984. "Artifacts from Later Pre-Islamic Occupation in Eastern Arabia", *Atlal* 8:165-169.

GROHMANN, A. 1914. "Göttersymbole und Symboltiere auf südarabischen Denkmälern", *Denkschriften der kaiserlichen Akademie der Wissenschaften in Wien, phil.-hist. Kl.* 58. Band, 1. Abhandlung, Vienna, p. 3-103.

GROHMANN, A. 1927. "Zur Archäologie Südarabiens", in D. Nielsen, ed., *Handbuch der altarabischen Altertumskunde I*, Nyt Nordisk Forlag, Copenhagen, p. 141-176.

HADACZEK, K. 1903. *Der Ohrschmuck der Griechen und Etrusker*, Abhandlungen des archäologischen-epigraphischen Seminars der Universität Wien XIV. Heft, Vienna.

HAERINCK, E. 1983. *La Céramique en Iran pendant la Période Parthe (ca. 250 av. J.C. a ca. 225 apres J.C.): Typologie, Chronologie et Distribution, IrAnt* Supplement II, Gent.

HAKEMI, A. 1972. *Catalogue de l'Exposition: LUT Xabis "Shahdad"*, Premier Symposium Annuel de la recherche Archéologique en Iran, Teheran.

HALLER, A. 1954. *Die Gräber und Grüfte von Assur, WVDOG* 65, Berlin.

HAMMOND, P. 1981. "Ein nabatäisches Weihrelief aus Petra", in G.H. Salies, ed., *Die Nabatäer*, Rheinisches Landesmuseum, Bonn, p. 27-60.

HANNESTAD, L. 1983. *The Hellenistic Pottery from Failaka, With a Survey of Hellenistic Pottery in the Near East*, Ikaros - The Hellenistic Settlements Vol. 2 (= *JASP* XVI:2), Aarhus.

HARLE, J.C. 1985. "Herakles Subduing the Horse(s) of Diomedes and Krsna Slaying the Demon-horse Kesin: a Common Iconographic Formula", in J. Schotsmans and M. Taddei, eds., *South Asian Archaeology 1983*, Naples, p. 641-652.

HARPER, P.O. 1978. *The Royal Hunter: Art of the Sasanian Empire*, The Asia Society, New York.

HIGGINS, R. 1980. *Greek and Roman Jewellery*, 2nd ed., Methuen & Co., London.

HOFFMANN, H. and P.F. DAVIDSON. 1965. *Greek Gold, Jewelry from the Age of Alexander*, Brooklyn Museum, New York.

JAMES, W.E. 1969. "On the Location of Gerrha", *AAW* 5/2:36-57.

JAMME, A. 1966. *Sabaean and Hasaean Inscriptions from Saudi Arabia*, Studi Semitici 23, Rome.

KOHL, P.L. 1974. *Seeds of Upheaval: The Production of Chlorite at Tepe Yahya and an Analysis of Commodity Production and Trade in Southwest Asia in the Mid-Third Millennium*, PhD. thesis, Harvard University, Cambridge.

KRAAY, C.M. and P.R.S. MOOREY. 1969. "Two Fifth Century Hoards from the Near East", *Revue Numismatique*, 6th ser. X:181-235.

KRÖGER, J. 1978. "Stucco", in P.O. Harper, *The Royal Hunter: Art of the Sasanian Empire*, Asia House, New York, p. 101-118.

LAMBERG-KARLOVSKY, C.C. 1970. *Excavations at Tepe Yahya, Iran, 1967-1969, Progress Report I*, Bulletin of the American School of Prehistoric Research 27, Cambridge.

LAMBERG-KARLOVSKY, C.C. 1988. "The 'Intercultural Style' Carved Vessels", *IrAnt* 23:45-95.

LAMBERG-KARLOVSKY, C.C. and M. TOSI. 1973. "Shahr-i Sokhta and Tepe Yahya: Tracks on the Earliest History of the Iranian Plateau", *EW* 23:21-53.

LOMBARD, P. 1979. *Aspects Culturels de la Péninsule d'Oman au Début du 1e Millénaire av. J.C.*, Mémoire de Maitrise, University of Paris 1, Paris.

LOMBARD, P. 1985. *L'Arabie Orientale a l'Age du Fer*, PhD. thesis, University of Paris 1, Paris.

LOMBARD, P. 1986. "Iron Age Dilmun: A reconsideration of City IV at Qal'at al-Bahrain", *BTA*:225-232.

LOMBARD, P. 1988. "The Salt Mine Site and the 'Hasaean Period' of Northeastern Arabia", *CNIP* 7: 116-135.

LOMBARD, P. and J.-F. SALLES. 1984. *La Nécropole de Janussan (Bahrain)*, *TMO* 6, Lyon.

LORIMER, J.G. 1908. *Gazetteer of the Persian Gulf, 'Oman, and Central Arabia, Vol. II, Geographical and Statistical*, Superintendent Government Printing, Calcutta.

LUKONIN, V.G. 1967. *Persia II*, Nagel, Geneva.

MANDAVILLE, J.P. 1963. "Thaj: A Pre-Islamic Site in Northeastern Arabia", *BASOR* 172:9-20.

MARSHALL, F.H. 1907. *Catalogue of the Finger Rings, Greek, Etruscan and Roman, in the Department of Antiquities of the British Museum*, London.

MASRY, A.H. 1974. *Prehistory in Northeastern Arabia: the Problem of Interregional Interaction*, Field Research Projects, Coconut Grove.

MAXWELL-HYSLOP, K.R. 1971. *Western Asiatic Jewellery c. 3000-612 B.C.*, Methuen & Co., London.

MCCLURE, H.A. 1971. *The Arabian Peninsula and Prehistoric Populations*, Field Research Projects, Coconut Grove.

MCDOWELL, R.H. 1935. *Stamped and Inscribed Objects from Seleucia on the Tigris*, Univ. of Michigan, Ann Arbor.

MIROSCHEDJI, P. DE. 1973. "Vases et objets en stéatites susiens du musée du Louvre", *DAFI* 3:9-80.

MORGAN, H. DE. 1905. "Recherches au Talyche Persan en 1901. Nécropoles des Ages du Bronze et du Fer", *MDP* VIII:251-342.

MORGAN, J. DE. 1905. "Trouvaille du Masque d'Argent", *MDP* VII:43-47.

MORRIS, R.W. 1975. "An Eighth Century Hoard from Eastern Arabia", *Coin Hoards* I.

NISSEN, H.J. 1970. "Grabung in den Quadraten K/L XII in Uruk-Warka", *BaM* 5:101-191.

NÖLDEKE, T. 1893. "Die von Guidi herausgegebene syrische Chronik", *Sitzungsberichte der Kaiserlichen Akademie der Wissenschaften, phil.-hist. Cl.* CXXVIII:1-48.

OATES, D. 1986. "Dilmun and the Late Assyrian Empire", *BTA*:428-434.

PARR, P.J., G.L. HARDING and J.E. DAYTON. 1972. "Preliminary Survey in N.W. Arabia, 1968", *Bulletin of the Institute of Archaeology* 10:23-61.

PÉZARD, M. and E. POTTIER. 1926. *Catalogue des Antiquités de la Susiane (Mission J. de Morgan)*, Musées Nationaux, Paris.

PHILLIPS, C.S. 1987. *Wadi Al Qawr, Fashgha 1. The Excavation of a Prehistoric Burial Structure in Ras Al Khaimah, U.A.E., 1986*, Univ. of Edinburgh, Dept. of Archaeology Project Paper No. 7, Edinburgh.

PIESINGER, C.M. 1983. *Legacy of Dilmun: The Roots of Ancient Maritime Trade in Eastern Coastal Arabia in the Fourth/Third Millennium B.C.*, Univ. Microfilms, Ann Arbor and London.

PIRENNE, J. 1977. *Corpus des Inscriptions et Antiquités Sud-Arabes*, Tome 1 - Section 2, Peeters, Louvain.

PITTMAN, H. 1984. *Art of the Bronze Age: Southeastern Iran, Western Central Asia, and the Indus Valley*, Metropolitan Museum of Art, New York.

PONGRATZ-LEISTEN, B. 1988. "Keramik der frühdynastischen Zeit aus der Grabungen in Uruk-Warka", *BaM* 19:177-319.

PORADA, E. 1948. *Corpus of Ancient Near Eastern Seals in North American Collections*, The Bollingen Series XIV, Washington.

PORADA, E. 1964. "Art of Iran, from the Prehistoric to the Sasanian Period", *7000 Years of Iranian Art*, Smithsonian Institution, Washington, p. 11-32.

PORADA, E. 1965. *The Art of Ancient Iran*, Crown, New York.

PORADA, E. 1967. "Of Deer, Bells, and Pomegranates", *IrAnt* 7:99-120.

POTTIER, M.-H. 1984. *Matériel Funéraire de la Bactriane Méridionale de l'Age du Bronze*, Éditions Recherche sur les Civilisations, Paris.

POTTS, D.T. 1980. *Tradition and Transformation: Tepe Yahya and the Iranian Plateau during the Third Millennium B.C.*, PhD. thesis, Harvard University, Cambridge.

POTTS, D.T. 1984. "Northeastern Arabia in the Later Pre-Islamic Era", *AOMIM*:85-144.

POTTS, D.T. 1986a "Eastern Arabia and the Oman Peninsula during the Late Fourth and Early Third Millennium B.C.", in U. Finkbeiner and W. Röllig, eds., *Gamdat Nasr - period or regional style?*, Beihefte zum Tübinger Atlas des Vorderen Orients, Reihe B, Nr. 62, Wiesbaden, p. 121-170.

POTTS, D.T. 1986b. "The Booty of Magan", *OrAnt* 25:271-285.

POTTS, D.T. in press a. *The Arabian Gulf in Antiquity*, Clarendon Press, Oxford.

POTTS, D.T. in press b. "The Chronology of the Archaeological Assemblages from the Head of the Arabian Gulf to the Arabian Sea (8000-1750 B.C.)", in R.W. Ehrich, ed., *Chronologies in Old World Archaeology*, Univ. of Chicago, Chicago.

POTTS, D.T., A.S. MUGHANNUM, J. FRYE, and D. SANDERS. 1978. "Preliminary Report on the Second Phase of the Eastern Province Survey 1397/1977", *Atlal* 2:7-28.

POTTS, T.F. n.d. "Foreign Stone Vessels of the late Third Millennium B.C. from Southern Mesopotamia: Questions of Origin and Mechanisms of Exchange", *Iraq*, in press.

RASHID, S.A. 1972. "Eine frühdynastische Statue von der Insel Tarut im Persischen Golf", *Gesellschaftsklassen im alten Zweistromland und in den angrenzenden Gebieten, XVIII. Rencontre Assyriologique Internationale*, Bayerische Akademie der Wissenschaften, phil.-hist. Kl., N.F. Heft 75, Serie A/6, Munich, p. 159-166.

RATHJENS, C. and H. VON WISSMANN. 1932. *Vorislamische Altertümer*, Hamburgische Universität Abhandlungen aus dem Gebiet der Auslandskunde Bd. 38, Reihe B. Bd. 19 (= Rathjens-v. Wissmannsche Südarabien-Reise Bd. 2), Hamburg.

RICCIARDI, R. VENCO. 1985. "Choche, Ceramica", *La Terra tra i Due Fiumi*, Il Quadrante Edizioni, Turin, p. 133-140.

RICE, M. 1985. *Search for the Paradise Land*, Longman, London and New York.

ROSCHINSKI, H.P. 1981. "Sprachen, Schriften und Inschriften in Nordwestarabien", in G.H. Salies, ed., *Die Nabatäer*, Rheinisches Landesmuseum, Bonn, p. 27-60.

SALLES, J.-F. 1986. "The Janussan necropolis and late first millennium B.C. burial customs in Bahrain", *BTA*: 445-461.

SORDINAS, A. 1973. *Contributions to the Prehistory of Saudi Arabia: II*, Field Research Projects, Coconut Grove.

SORDINAS, A. 1978. *Contributions to the Prehistory of Saudi Arabia: III*, Field Research Projects, Coconut Grove.

SPELEERS, L. 1917. *Catalogue des Intailles et Empreintes Orientales des Musées Royaux du Cinquantenaire*, Vromant, Brussels.

SPYCKET, A. 1981. *La Statuaire du Proche-Orient Ancien*, Handbuch der Orientalistik, Siebente Abteilung, I. Band, 2. Abschnitt B, Lfg. 2, Leiden-Köln.

STARR, R.F.S. 1937. *Nuzi*, Harvard University Press, Cambridge.

STRONACH, D. 1978. *Pasargadae*, Clarendon Press, Oxford.

STROMMENGER, E. 1967. *Gefässe aus Uruk von der neubabylonischen Zeit bis zu den Sasaniden*, Ausgrabungen der Deutschen Forschungsgemeinschaft in Uruk-Warka Bd. 7, Berlin.

STUCKY, R.A. 1983. *Ras Shamra, Leukos Limen, die nach-ugaritische Be-*

siedlung von Ras Shamra, Geuthner, Paris.

TAHA, M.Y. 1982-83. "The Archaeology of the Arabian Gulf during the First Millennium B.C.", *Al-Rafidan* III-IV:75-87.

THILO, U. 1957. *Die Ortsnamen in der altarabischen Poesie*, Harrassowitz, Wiesbaden.

THOMPSON, D. 1976. *Stucco from Chal Tarkhan-Eshqabad near Rayy*, Aris & Phillips, Warminster.

THORVILDSEN, K. 1963. "Gravrøser på Umm an-Nar (Burial Cairns on Umm an-Nar)", *Kuml 1962*: 191-219.

TOSI, M. 1976. "The Dating of the Umm an-Nar Culture and a Proposed Sequence for Oman in the Third Millennium BC", *JOS* 2:81-92.

TOSI, M. 1983. "Development, Continuity and Cultural Change in the Stratigraphical Sequence of Shahr-i Sokhta", in M. Tosi, ed., *Prehistoric Sistan 1*, IsMEO, Rome, p. 127-179.

TURNER, G. 1973. "South Arabian Gold Jewellery", *Iraq* 35:127-139.

VALTZ, E. 1985. "Seleucia, Ceramica", *La Terra tra i Due Fiumi*, Il Quadrante Edizioni, Turin, p. 121-124.

VAN BEEK, G.W. 1969. *Hajar Bin Humeid: Investigations at a Pre-Islamic Site in South Arabia*, Johns Hopkins Press, Baltimore.

VANDEN BERGHE, L. 1955-56. "De Beschilderde Ceramiek in Voor-Azie van de oudste Tijden tot ± 2000 voor onze Jaartelling: Studie van Stijl, Ontwikkeling, Verspreiding en Wetenschappelijk Belang (Tweede deel)", *Gentse bijdragen tot de Kunwstgeschiedenis* XVI:5-54.

VÉRTESALJI, P.P. and S. KOLBUS. "Review of Protodynastic Development in Babylonia", *Mesopotamia* 20:53-109.

VOGT, B. 1985. "The Umm an-Nar Tomb A at Hili North: A preliminary report on three seasons of excavation, 1982-1984", *AUAE* 4:20-37.

VOGT, B. and U. FRANKE-VOGT. 1987. *Shimal 1985/1986, Excavations of the German Archaeological Mission in Ras Al-Khaimah, U.A.E., A Preliminary Report, BBVO* 8, Berlin.

VOLLENWEIDER, M.-L. 1967. *Catalogue Raisonné des Sceaux Cylindres et Intailles, Vol. I*, Musée d'Art et d'Histoire de Geneve, Geneva.

VOLLENWEIDER, M.-L. 1983. *Catalogue Raisonné des Sceaux, Cylindres, Intailles et Camées, Vol. III*, Musée d'Art et d'Histoire de Geneve, Von Zabern, Mainz.

VON DER OSTEN, H.H. 1934. *Ancient Oriental Seals in the Collection of Mr. Edward T. Newell, OIP* XXII, Chicago.

VON DER OSTEN, H.H. 1936. *Ancient Oriental Seals in the Collection of Mrs. Agnes Baldwin Brett, OIP* XXXVII, Chicago.

VON DER OSTEN, H.H. 1957. *Altorientalische Siegelsteine der Sammlung Hans Silvius von Aulock*, Studia Ethnographica Upsaliensia XIII, Uppsala.

WALTERS, H.B. 1926. *Catalogue of the Engraved Gems and Cameos, Greek, Etruscan and Roman, in the British Museum*, London.

WEISGERBER, G. 1981. "Mehr als Kupfer in Oman - Ergebnisse der Expedition 1981", *Der Anschnitt* 33:174-263.

WHITCOMB, D. 1984. "Qasr-i Abu Nasr and the Gulf", *AOMIM*: 331-337.

WHITCOMB, D. 1987. "Bushire and the Angali Canal", *Mesopotamia* 22:311-336.

WINNETT, F.V. and W.L. REED. 1970. *Ancient Records from North Arabia*, Univ. of Toronto, Toronto.

WOOLLEY, C.L. 1934. *Ur Excavations II, The Royal Cemetery*, British Museum and University Museum, London.

WOOLLEY, SIR L. 1955. *Ur Excavations IV, The Early Periods*, Vol. II, British Museum and University Museum, Philadelphia.

WOOLLEY, SIR L. 1962. *Ur Excavations IX, The Neo-Babylonian and Persian Periods*, British Museum and University Museum, London.

YULE, P. and G. WEISGERBER. 1988. *Samad ash-Shan: Excavation of the Pre-Islamic Cemeteries, Preliminary Report 1988*, Bochum.

ZARINS, J. 1978. "Steatite Vessels in the Riyadh Museum", *Atlal* 2:65-93.

ZARINS, J., A.S. MUGHANNUM and M. KAMAL. 1984. "Excavations at Dhahran South - The Tumuli Field (208-92), 1403 A.H. 1983. A Preliminary Report", *Atlal* 8:25-54.

List of Figures